far east
down east

far east
down east

*Maine's freshest foods spiced
with Asia's finest flavors*

A COOKBOOK BY
BRUCE de**MUSTCHINE**

PHOTOGRAPHY BY
GLENN SCOTT

DOWN EAST BOOKS
CAMDEN, MAINE

ISBN 0-89272-589-3

Library of Congress Catalog Card Number: 2002114907

Book design by Harrah Lord, Yellow House Studio

Printed in China

OGP

5 4 3 2 1

Down East Books / Camden, Maine

Book orders: (800) 766-1670

www.downeastbooks.com

contents

acknowledgments

This book has been many years in the making, with tips from chefs in Japan, China, India, Singapore, Hong Kong, and throughout New England. I thank them all for their help and assistance.

Special thanks must be given to John and Tori Parrott for reviewing each and every recipe; to Richard Crammer for his valuable assistance with the digital photography process; to Edith, my wife who not only took on the daunting task of cleaning up after each photo shoot but endured all the trials of each and every dish; and to Oliver Coolidge for his careful review of all of the content. Thanks are also due to Terence Gleeson and Hank Totzke for their assistance in supplying photographic props.

Special thanks and acknowledgment go to the Edgecomb Potters Guild, Edgecomb, Maine, who kindly lent their exquisite Japanese-inspired glazed porcelains for photography on pages 40, 41, 44, 59, 73, 77, and 108.

For the past thirty years I have traveled the world both for business and pleasure. Much of my travel has been to the Far East, where I was taught to cook in Hong Kong, Malaysia, Thailand, Singapore, Penang, China, Indonesia, and Japan.

My interest in food, particularly Asian food, has been a lifelong passion. Now my traveling days are fewer, and for more than thirteen years I have lived on the Atlantic coast, in northern Massachusetts. Here I have an abundant supply of fresh seafood and a harvest of fruits and vegetables equal to any other area in this great country. Over these years my passion for the spices of Asia, blended with locally caught seafood, cranberries and other fruit, vegetables, and New England's maple syrup have fused in my Newburyport kitchen into an exciting palette of flavors.

This book is a selection of my favorite recipes, ones that I have modified and adapted to take advantage of readily available New England ingredients. These are dishes I cook for my family and friends using lobsters, sea scallops, native Maine shrimp, cod, and mussels laced together with chiles, lemongrass, fresh ginger, and the spices and sauces of the Far East.

My Life Started Down Under

New Zealand is the country of my birth. I am the first child of a World War II soldier from Waipawa (Maori for "village by the river"). This is a small country town on the banks of the Tukituki River in the southern part of Hawkes Bay on North Island. North of town lies the agricultural and horticultural center of Hastings, which became my home in the early 1950s. This area of New Zealand is covered with thick, rich alluvial soil that produces vast quantities and varieties of fruits and vegetables and exceptional wines.

As a boy, to supplement my allowance, I worked in the fields with my friends picking plump red tomatoes, cutting asparagus before dawn, and bending down to ground level for hours of backbreaking bean and pea picking. As the seasons progressed, work was available harvesting apples, peaches, apricots, cherries, raspberries, strawberries, red currants, and grapes. The whole community was alive with the activities of a long harvest time, and the air was full of aromas emanating from the factories that turned the produce into tomato ketchup, strawberry jam, and wine. Huge freezers were built to hold fruits and vegetables before sending them off to the markets of the world. Friends and family worked in the factories, as did I when I was seventeen for several weeks through my summer vacation.

No exotic flavors ever appeared in the preparation of food in my family home. Our meals consisted of lamb or mutton and the fruits and vegetables of the area. Spices were not generally used. Our food was basic New Zealand "tucker." The lamb or mutton was always roasted first, usually on a Sunday, and served with roasted vegetables and boiled greens. For the rest of the week, the remaining meat was served as shepherd's pie or cold slices with salads, or made into sandwiches. The only condiment available, which we used on almost everything, was tomato sauce made and bottled in the city by Watties* and produced from the very tomatoes that I had spent hours harvesting.

Once or twice a week we would have something different, usually at the end of the week when the lamb was finished. On Fridays it would be fish and chips, Saturday a chicken. But Thursdays was the day my sister and I tried at all costs to avoid eating the evening meal at home. This was the day our mother cooked the only meal containing spices of any kind. This was when she prepared the one meal she thought my father longed for ever since he had returned to New Zealand at the end of World War II.

My father served five years in the New Zealand army stationed in North Africa as part of General Montgomery's Eighth Army. Heading homeward for New Zealand in 1945, the troopship, carrying some 1,200 soldiers from Australia and New Zealand, encountered engine problems in the Indian Ocean, off the southeastern tip of India. After floundering for eight days, the ship was eventually towed to Ceylon (now known as Sri Lanka) and into the port of Colombo. The men on board spent the next three months waiting for spare parts to arrive. They lived both on and off the ship. As a result they were able to enjoy the wonderful culture of the Ceylonese and in particular feasting on the incredible foods of this spice-laden island. Their taste buds were tantalized by seafood and goat curries made from dozens of different spices that were pounded together daily. These were combined with garlic and onions and simmered in the milk of the local coconuts and all mopped up with delicious hoppers (thin, round bread). My father, bless his soul, fell in love with the flavors and textures of this, his first experience of Asian cooking.

* The J. Watties Canneries Ltd, known simply as "Watties," processed all sorts of vegetables.
The company today is part of a huge conglomerate, and the Watties logo exists no more.

A year after arriving back in New Zealand, my father met and married my mother, and a year later I was born. Family life became the order of the day, and my mother settled into cooking for the four of us and running the home. At some point my father's experiences in the war were revealed along with recollections of the meals he'd enjoyed in Colombo. In an attempt to please her husband, Mum searched the only three cookbooks she owned, and—bingo—there it was: curried sausages. And so the Thursday night ritual began.

The meal was carefully prepared according to the detailed instructions in *Aunt Daisy's Cook Book* and placed on the table in front of us: gray sausages lying in a canary yellow curry sauce in which floated pieces of onion. My father, being a gentleman in every sense of the word, ate the sausages; my sister and I suffered them. On more than one occasion I was known to capture one of the offending beasts and hide it in a napkin in my lap, to be disposed of later in the evening. My sister would plunge her piece of sausage into a glass of water before eating it to remove as much of the curry as possible. At the end of each meal, Dad would declare, "Not bad, dear. . . . It's not as good as I had in Colombo. I don't know what you do that's different. . . . Maybe next time it will be better." It never was.

Sadly, my father died in 1973, before he had a chance to rediscover the flavors of the Ceylon he knew and before I could prepare for him the meals I learned to cook after leaving New Zealand on my personal voyage of discovery.

My Quest to Discover the Flavors of the Far East

It was in 1971 that I left New Zealand to travel the world. As the plane lifted off from Auckland, headed for Fiji, I had no idea how soon I would taste the flavors of a real curry.

Two hours into the flight we ran into a tropical storm the likes of which I have never endured since, even after flying countless thousands of miles during the past three decades. The aircraft bounced so violently that I thought my venture into the world would start and finish in the South Pacific. When we did eventually land, the aircraft was unable to continue; it had sustained sufficient damage to prohibit another takeoff.

My seatmate throughout this ordeal was an elderly Indian woman dressed in a beautiful peacock blue sari who was as frightened as the rest of us. We could not communicate, because I did not speak Hindi and she did not speak English, but in a gesture to comfort her, I held out my hand, to which she clung very tightly until we taxied to the terminal. As I collected my baggage, my traveling companion's son shook my hand and thanked me for being a comfort to his mother. He asked if I would come to their home to celebrate her safe arrival back on the islands. I had no particular plans, so I said yes. That is how I started my discovery of the flavors of the Far East.

The entire family of nine and I bundled into a van and traveled twenty dusty miles to their home. As we rode, Vinod, the eldest son, explained to me how the Indians had been brought to the Fiji Islands by the British to work as laborers on the sugar plantations. "Now the Indians outnumber the locals and run the country," he told me.

As I was ushered into their home, the aroma of spices permeated the air. These new fragrances were so exotic and so intoxicating that I immediately knew this was what my father had discovered twenty-five years earlier. I did not even need to taste the prepared food to know and understand. The aromas tantalized my taste buds with a promise of great flavors to follow, and when the food was served—rich, creamy sauces the color of saffron and paprika, spiced with cloves, chiles, mustard seeds, coriander, cardamom, and ginger—I was in heaven. I ate until I could hold no more. From that day on, I have taken it as a personal challenge to learn and understand all there is to know about the flavors of the Far East.

Following my enforced, brief visit to the Fiji Islands, I continued east to Hawaii, then New York, and finally London. I had planned to work somewhere in the British Isles and sought employment as soon as I got over my jet lag. Within a week, I was offered a position in an advertising agency on the outskirts of the city. On my first day of employment, Wiggy, my new boss and now my longtime friend, took me into London's West End, first to a trade show, then out for dinner. With no prompting from me, we went to a restaurant called Veraswarmy's, on Regent Street. (Unfortunately, it no longer exists.)

Here haute cuisine from India was served in palatial surroundings: marble floors and columns, mirrored walls, huge ceiling fans, enormous palm trees in glazed ceramic pots. The staff were in exotic costumes, as if they had just come from a Hollywood film set. It was breathtaking. And the aromas were simply overwhelming—tantalizing fragrances created by simmering blended spices in coconut milk and yogurt. We ate *goojaas*, a puffy lamb appetizer; vegetable *bhajias*, huge, ballooning *poorie* with potato and spinach blended with subtle spices, and a chicken *biranee* garnished with gossamer-thin silver foil that had melted over the grains of saffron yellow basmati rice.

What a contrast between this feast and the one I had enjoyed in Fiji four weeks earlier. The presentation and the decor were as different as chalk and cheese—yet the cooking styles were identical. The textures and colors were alike, and the magnificent flavors came from the same marriage of spices and vegetables that has fascinated civilization for thousands of years.

And now, here I am living in New England, in one of the very ports from which clipper ships once sailed for the Far East and returned with spices amongst their cargo. It is here that my love of these flavors has been enriched by the bounty of local harvests: shellfish, berries, vegetables, maple syrup, and other delights.

My introduction to the fresh local fare started very quickly. I arrived in Newburyport two days before Thanksgiving in 1989 and was invited to share the holiday with some dear friends. I was told that everyone usually contributed a dish, so I set off to discover what was available. It wasn't long before I found the local fish market and lobster pound. Coming home laden with fresh lobsters, I set about creating what has become one of my favorite dishes—lobster bisque. After taking the meat from the bodies, tails, and claws, I simmered the lobster shells for two days to create the rich broth. Needless to say, the result was terrific.

The local seafood and produce soon became the staples for all that I love to cook. And I am still discovering ways to blend the flavors of this part of the world with the seasonings of the Far East that I love so well. The journey just keeps on going!

What You Will Find in This Book

The objective of this book, my fifth on the subject of Asian cooking, is to show just how simple it is to cook the harvests of New England while utilizing the style and flavors of Asia to create a unique Far East/Down East cuisine. Every recipe has been tested and refined in my Newburyport kitchen.

Exploring the whys and wherefores of cooking is one of my passions; kitchen simplicity is another. I've never found it necessary to overcomplicate the preparation of food. You'll find that all my recipes can be prepared in the average kitchen using ingredients from local supermarkets, farm stands, or lobster pounds—no fuss, no mystique, just rewarding, creative food.

The armory of any modern American kitchen dispenses with the hours of preparation that Asian cooking could easily demand. Working without the large staff found in most Asian kitchens, I have accumulated a few mechanical helpmates and other cookware, and I now recommend them to you.

An electric blender is a must. Mixers, toaster ovens, microwave ovens, grills, hobs (gas rings or burners), and rotisseries will also do the job, however non-ethnic they may seem.

Tandoori food, usually cooked in the famous Indian clay oven, can be convincingly and enjoyably cooked in a regular oven or under a grill after being carefully marinated in a yogurt and spice sauce.

A wok is considered by some to be indispensable for authentic Chinese cooking, though a deep skillet and high heat serve equally well. Buy a Chinese bamboo steamer from an Asian market or a store that carries imported cookware. If that's not feasible, though, you'll get equally good results from a conventional steamer.

Continuing the Art of Cooking

Variety is truly the spice of life.

As I traveled the great countries of Asia, I noticed that one aspect of the cooking of each country remains the same: a dish varies greatly from one kitchen to another and from one province to the next. Whether it is Chicken Korma in India, Pad Thai in Thailand, or Beef Rendang in Indonesia, the color, texture, and flavors vary, although the name stays the same.

Cooking, much like the different dialects spoken throughout any country, changes from one city to the next and from one region to another. Dishes are "interpreted" depending largely on the ingredients available and the cooking methods employed. Substitutions are made in one kitchen as a result of the shortage of an ingredient; if the resulting change is enjoyed, it soon becomes the defended standard.

Cooking is an art, not a science. There is no formula for painters to mix colors on their palette and apply them to a canvas to express the image in their mind. Cooking is the same. Ingredients are your pigments. Their preparation, with the addition of heat, is the creative process that results in food to be enjoyed. We are fortunate today to be able to select ingredients from every corner of the globe, blend them in our twenty-first-century kitchens, and enjoy food very close to the original—if an original could ever be found!

What I do in my kitchen is to cook creatively, and I hope you will do so in yours. Use fresh ingredients, blend the spices and sauces from the Far East, utilize the equipment you own, and substitute whenever you feel the need or necessity. Take pride in the fact that you are continuing the evolution of the art of cooking!

So, here's to good cooking or, as the Maoris say, *Pai tao*.

flavors
of the far east

One of the magical aspects of Asian cooking is the flavor imparted by a small selection of spices, sauces, fruits, and nuts. Without these pungent, zesty, and many times fiery taste sensations, Asian food would be somewhat bland. It is the combination of fresh prime ingredients and these unique flavors that gives the region its culinary character—a character not experienced in any other part of the globe. There literally is no substitution for the flavors of Asia.

Following are brief descriptions of the Asian ingredients referenced in this book. Many are now readily available in supermarkets; others may need to be purchased in specialty stores or Asian markets or from the continually changing list of on-line retailers. An excellent resource for dried spices and herbs is Penzey's Spices: www.penzeys.com

Red and Green Chiles: More articles and books have been written about chiles, also called chile peppers, than any other spice. Chiles come in dozens of different sizes, colors, and degrees of heat and provide the basis of numerous adventures. Originally from South America, they were introduced into Asia in the sixteenth century and are now the most significant flavor throughout the area.

In all the recipes in this book, I use Thai chiles (*Prik ki nu*), for no other reason than they are my personal favorite. They can be readily purchased green or red. Green chiles are unripened and have a distinctive "green" flavor. Always remember that whatever chile you use, the hot part is the seeds. This is where the real punch and heat come from.

Crushed Dried Chile: These vary in heat from one processor to another and contain both the dried flesh and seeds of red chiles.

Chili Powder: Simply, crushed dried chiles that have been milled to a coarse powder.

Black Peppercorns: The world's most popular spice, black peppercorns added heat to Asian foods before the chile was introduced in the sixteenth century.

Cinnamon: The finest cinnamon comes from Sri Lanka; it is the inner bark of a native laurel tree. After being cut from the tree, the inner bark naturally rolls into quills, or sticks, as it dries. More common in the United States is Chinese cinnamon, which is the bark of the cassia tree, a close cousin of the laurel. Cinnamon is the "first" recorded spice and is used extensively in Chinese, Vietnamese, and Korean cooking.

Ground Cinnamon: This is basically ground cinnamon sticks. It does not have the fresh, distinctive flavor of the whole quills.

Sesame Seeds: Sesame oil is extracted from these seeds. They are usually toasted before being used and have a wonderful nutty flavor.

Cumin: Cumin is available as seeds or in ground form. A member of the parsley family, it is a widely used spice throughout the Far East. The flavor is bittersweet.

Turmeric: Only ground turmeric is available in North America. A member of the ginger family, turmeric is a bright yellow rhizome that is used fresh in the Far East.

Coriander: Available as seeds and in ground form, coriander is almost as widely used as cumin. This is the seed of cilantro, a member of the parsley family that is a popular fresh seasoning.

Daikon: Japanese radish, or Chinese turnip, is a huge root vegetable, sometimes up to twenty inches long and three inches in diameter. It is less peppery than the traditional salad radish. A staple vegetable in Asian cooking, daikon is used in soups, stir-fries, and sauces. When thinly sliced, it is used as the basis of food sculpture in China and Japan.

Galangal: Inedible as it is, the rhizome of the galangal plant lends a flavor unlike any other. The woodlike rhizome is added to soups and stews and is removed before eating. The plant is a member of the ginger family.

Shredded Coconut and Coconut Milk: Throughout Asia the coconut palm provides a wide range of products. The fronds are used as matting, baskets, and roofing. The husks are woven into rope and floor coverings. Palm sugar is made from the extracted sap, and the juice provides a refreshing drink. It is the innards of the nut that are processed to provide coconut milk and flesh. The innards are also sold as shredded coconut in the United States and used mainly in desserts. The milk is the basis of dishes from the southern tip of Indonesia to the northern reaches of India.

Most supermarkets carry at least one variety of canned coconut milk. Make sure it is unsweetened. Sometimes it is clearly labeled as such; if not, check the ingredients list. Sweetened versions are used exclusively in the making of "tropical cocktails." You can make your own coconut milk by putting 2 cups of shredded coconut in a blender with 2 cups of hot water and blending for one minute. Strain the liquid and discard the solids. (It is fine to use the readily available sweetened shredded coconut for this purpose.)

Ginger: Ginger, an edible rhizome, is my favorite of all Asian flavors. It can be chopped, grated, sliced, or squeezed. It imparts a zesty, distinguished tang to foods. Ground ginger is available but *cannot* be substituted where fresh ginger is called for.

When buying fresh ginger, only purchase plump roots with a sheen to the skin. If the ginger looks wrinkled and dried out, leave it.

Pickled Ginger: This very thinly sliced ginger packed in sweetened vinegar is used as a condiment. It is mostly pink, the color coming from a natural reaction between the vinegar and the ginger. (Some is a light brown, however, because exporters did not think that the pink color would be acceptable in the West and altered the recipe to prevent the natural "pinking" of the ginger.)

Wasabi: Wasabi powder is the pungently hot base for wasabi paste, which accompanies sashimi and sushi in Japanese restaurants. Wasabi must be used with respect. Adding a little water to the dried, powdered wasabi root makes the paste. Wasabi is part of the horseradish family and is now being grown in the Pacific Northwest and in New Zealand.

Lemongrass: This "grass" from Southeast Asia is now grown commercially in Florida and California. It has an intensely fragrant flavor, somewhere between a freshly cut lawn and lemons. It is either finely chopped and added to dishes or bruised and added as large pieces, which are removed before eating.

Hoisin Sauce: This popular condiment adds a distinctive tang to barbecued foods throughout China. It is made from fermented soybeans, garlic, ginger, chiles, and sesame oil. It can be used in the cooking process or as a table condiment.

Mango Chutney: Made mainly in India from mangoes, vinegar, spices, and chiles, this ubiquitous condiment is delicious with fried foods and curries. In Great Britain and most of the British Commonwealth, mango chutney has become almost as popular as ketchup is in the States.

Fish Sauce: In Thailand it's called *nam pla*, in Vietnam *nuoc mam*, and in Roman times *liquamen*. In all cases the same ingredients give this sauce the same complex, salty flavor. The sauce is produced by layering fish and salt in vats and collecting the liquid that forms as the mixture ferments. The resulting pungent liquor should be used sparingly. There is no substitute for the unique flavor.

Soy Sauce: This staple throughout the whole of the Far East has also become a staple in the American kitchen. Soy sauce is as complex as wine, and there are thousands of varieties, but fundamentally all are made from a mixture of soybeans, wheat, and water, which is fermented and distilled. There are three major types:

> **Light**—Delicate and subtle in flavor, ideal for dipping sauces.
> **Medium**—Saltier and darker than the light varieties, an all-purpose soy sauce. The soy sauce used in all *Far East/Down East* recipes unless otherwise stated.
> **Heavy**—Medium soy sauce to which molasses has been added, making it thicker and heavier. Ideal for marinades and stews.

Japanese and Chinese soy sauces are very much the same. Centuries ago, the Chinese taught the Japanese the art of making soy sauce, including Tamari. True Tamari is brewed and distilled without the wheat and is rare today, even in Japan. It is commonly mislabeled in the U.S., and high prices are paid for what is basically "soy sauce."

Rice Vinegar: Also called rice wine vinegar, this light-flavored liquid is produced by the souring of rice wine. It can be used as you would use any vinegar, but it is most appropriate in Asian dishes that call for vinegar.

Mustard Seeds: These seeds range in color from black to a purplish brown and are used mainly in Indian cooking.

Saffron: This is the most expensive spice in the world. It takes about a hundred thousand crocus blooms to produce enough stigmas to get one pound of saffron. The saffron threads add a musky aroma to food but are most prized for the rich golden color they impart. The best saffron comes from Kashmir. The most readably available in the United States comes from Mancha, Spain.

Cardamom: Each straw-colored pod contains ten to sixteen seeds; these are the treasures. The seeds should be removed and lightly crushed to release their eucalyptus-like fragrance and flavor.

Sesame Oil: Sesame oil is sought after purely for its fragrant, nutty flavor, for which it is added to soups and rice just before serving. It is not generally used for cooking. Its flavor is utilized to its best in dressings and dipping sauces. The process of toasting the seeds and extracting the oil is tedious and accounts for the high price of the finished product.

Oyster Sauce: From Canton via Hong Kong to America, oyster sauce is the flavor most associated with Chinese-American food. It is made in southern China from oysters, salt, and water. Caramel coloring gives the sauce its dark brown hue.

Sweet Chile Sauce: This is Thailand's tomato ketchup! Made from chiles, sugar, salt, and vinegar, it is somewhat sweet and very popular. It can be used as a stir-fry sauce but is best as a table condiment.

Curry Paste: Curry pastes from India and Thailand have become more readily available throughout the United States. There are dozens of different pastes, all with greatly varying flavor bases. Here are three:

    green curry paste (Thailand)
    Vindaloo paste (India)
    hot curry paste (India)

starters & snacks

SAIGON SHRIMP CAKES

Saigon Shrimp Cakes

SERVES 4
COOKING TIME: 10 MINUTES

3 scallions
1¹⁄₂ pounds fresh uncooked shrimp
1 tablespoon fish sauce
3 sprigs parsley
1 teaspoon salt
¹⁄₂ teaspoon freshly ground black pepper
1 tablespoon flour
4 tablespoons vegetable oil

PREPARATION

Coarsely chop 2 of the scallions and place in a food processor. Finely slice the third scallion and set aside. Peel the shrimp and add to the scallions in the food processor. Add the fish sauce, parsley, salt, and pepper, and process until the mixture is smooth but still has a few chunks of shrimp. Add the finely sliced scallion and process briefly.

Sprinkle the flour onto a flat work surface. Turn out the shrimp mixture and form into 8 small, flat cakes. Chill for about 30 minutes in the refrigerator.

COOKING

Heat the oil in a large, heavy skillet. Add the cakes, a few at a time, and cook until golden brown. Turn and brown the other side. Remove and drain on paper towels. Serve hot.

Steamed Picnic

Serving steamed lobster, shrimp, or crab with spicy dipping sauces is a simple way to give these traditional dishes an authentic Asian flavor. Personally, I love lobster cold and served this way. And shrimp is just as tasty and a lot easier to peel.

The cooking of the lobster, shrimp, or crab, and the amount you use will depend on your own tried and proven methods. As the crustaceans are steaming, prepare at least two of the following dipping sauces.

EACH SAUCE RECIPE SERVES 4.

Garlic & Chile Dipping Sauce

3 cloves garlic
2 fresh red chiles
juice of 1 lemon
3 tablespoons soy sauce
2 teaspoons sugar
1 tablespoon fish sauce

PREPARATION

Chop the garlic very finely. Seed and finely chop the chiles. Mix the chopped garlic and chiles with the lemon juice, soy sauce, sugar, and fish sauce. Pour into a dipping bowl.

Ginger & Lime
Dipping Sauce

2-inch piece fresh ginger

1 clove garlic

juice of 1 lime

2 tablespoons unsweetened coconut milk

2 tablespoons water

3 teaspoons soy sauce

1 teaspoon rice vinegar

1 teaspoon sugar

2 teaspoons fish sauce

PREPARATION

Peel and thinly slice the ginger, then finely chop. Crush and finely chop the garlic. Set aside.

In a small saucepan, combine the lime juice, coconut milk, and water; bring to a gentle boil. Add the soy sauce and rice vinegar. Stir while adding the sugar; continue to stir until it is dissolved. Remove the pan from the heat and allow to cool.

Add the chopped ginger, chopped garlic, and fish sauce. Stir well, then pour into a dipping bowl.

Tomato & Soy
Dipping Sauce

3 scallions

3 cloves garlic

1 cup ketchup

2 tablespoons soy sauce

4 teaspoons prepared horseradish

1 tablespoon fish sauce

PREPARATION

Finely slice the scallions. Crush and chop the garlic. Combine all the ingredients; then pour into a dipping bowl.

Shrimp Toast

Small, sweet Maine shrimp are ideal for this dish, but any type of shrimp may be used.

SERVES 4
COOKING TIME: ABOUT 15 MINUTES

4 slices bread

½ pound fresh uncooked shrimp

1 tablespoon butter

3 tablespoons vegetable oil

1 teaspoon salt

1 teaspoon freshly ground black pepper

half a small cucumber

3 tablespoons fish sauce

1 tablespoon maple syrup

1 scallion

1 clove garlic

4 leaves lettuce

mint leaves for garnish

PREPARATION

Cut the crusts off the bread. Peel and devein the shrimp. In an electric blender or food processor, combine the deveined shrimp, the butter, 1 tablespoon of the oil, and the salt and pepper to a smooth paste. With a knife, firmly spread the paste onto the slices of bread.

Slice the cucumber; set aside. Mix together the fish sauce and the maple syrup. Finely slice the scallion and finely chop the garlic. Stir them into the fish sauce mixture, and set aside.

COOKING

Heat the remaining 2 tablespoons oil in a deep skillet. Place 1 or 2 slices of the bread, paste-side down, in the hot oil, and cook until golden brown. Turn over and cook until the bread just starts to brown. Drain on paper towels. Repeat with the remaining bread. Cut the cooked bread diagonally into quarters.

ASSEMBLY

Place a lettuce leaf on each of 4 plates and arrange 4 quarters of bread on top of each leaf. Garnish with the cucumber slices and mint leaves. Serve the fish sauce separately to be used as desired.

SHRIMP TOAST

Shrimp & Lobster Mousse

SERVES 6
COOKING TIME: 30 MINUTES
CHILL FOR 1 HOUR

½ **pound unpeeled cooked shrimp**

1 **small cooked lobster**

2 **egg whites**

2 **cups heavy cream**

1 **small yellow onion**

1 **clove garlic**

1 **teaspoon fish sauce**

1 **teaspoon chili powder**

½ **teaspoon freshly ground black pepper**

6 **to 8 chives**

1 **lemon**

butter, for ramekins

PREPARATION

Preheat the oven to 350° F. Set aside 6 shrimp for garnish. Peel the remaining shrimp and transfer to a food processor.

Remove the meat from the tail of the cooked lobster and cut into 6 medallions; set aside. Remove the remaining meat from the lobster and add to the food processor.

Beat the egg whites until they are stiff; set aside. Pour the heavy cream into the food processor with the shrimp and lobster. Peel the onion and cut into quarters; add to the food processor. Add the garlic, fish sauce, chili powder, and ground pepper. Process to a smooth paste. Fold in the beaten egg whites.

Rinse and cut the chives into 3-inch lengths. Using a lemon zester, remove just the yellow layer of the lemon rind. Set aside this zest and the chives to be used as garnish.

Lightly butter 6 ramekins. Pour the shrimp mixture to within half an inch of the top of each. Place the ramekins in a baking dish, and add water to halfway up the sides of the ramekins.

COOKING
Place the baking dish in the preheated oven and bake for 30 minutes, by which time the mousse should have risen and started to brown. Remove from the oven. Allow to cool on a baking rack, then refrigerate for at least 1 hour. Garnish with the reserved lobster medallions and shrimp, and the chives and lemon zest.

Shrimp & Pork Spring Rolls

These spring rolls require no cooking and can contain any combination of salad items, fresh herbs, shrimp, pork, or chicken.

SERVES 4 TO 6
PREPARATION TIME: 15 MINUTES

1 pound cooked, shelled shrimp
1/2 pound cooked pork tenderloin
1/2 teaspoon freshly ground black pepper
1/4 teaspoon salt
half a head romaine lettuce
1 cup fresh basil leaves
1 cup fresh mint leaves
2 fresh red chiles
10 chives
1 cup bean sprouts
2 tablespoons vegetable oil
2 cups water
2 teaspoons fish sauce
20 rice paper wrappers

PREPARATION
Cut the shrimp in half lengthwise. Shred the pork and season it with the pepper and salt. Remove the heart from the lettuce; wash and separate the heart leaves and cut them into 3-inch-long pieces. Wash the basil and mint leaves. Seed and finely chop the chiles. Wash the chives and cut into 3-inch lengths. Wash and drain the bean sprouts.

SHRIMP & PORK SPRING ROLLS

ASSEMBLY

Dip the rice paper wrappers into hot water for a few seconds until they become soft and pliable. Place the softened wrappers on a few paper towels. In the center of each wrapper, arrange 1 or 2 pieces of lettuce, then some halved shrimp, pork, basil and mint leaves, chopped chiles, chives, and bean sprouts. Fold over one of the long edges of the wrapper, then fold over the ends tightly. Now roll the whole thing into a traditional spring roll shape, as shown in the photograph.

Serve at room temperature with the following dipping sauce.

Dipping Sauce

1 fresh red chile

1 clove garlic

juice of half a lime

4 tablespoons unsweetened coconut milk

2 tablespoons water

1 teaspoon rice vinegar

1 teaspoon sugar

2 tablespoons fish sauce

PREPARATION

Seed and finely chop the chile. Crush and finely chop the garlic. Set aside.

In a small saucepan, combine the lime juice, coconut milk, and the water; bring to a gentle boil. Add the rice vinegar. Stir while adding the sugar; continue to stir until it is dissolved. Remove from the heat and allow to cool.

Add the reserved chopped chile and garlic and the fish sauce. Stir well, then pour into a dipping bowl and serve.

Chile Oysters

SERVES 4
PREPARATION TIME: 15 MINUTES
4 TO 6 OYSTERS PER PERSON

2 fresh red chiles

1 scallion

1 clove garlic

1 teaspoon sugar

2 teaspoons white wine vinegar

3 tablespoons soy sauce

PREPARATION

Shuck the oysters and cut the meat away from the shell. Leave each oyster sitting in a half shell. Divide the oysters among 4 serving plates.

Seed and finely slice the chiles. Finely slice the scallion. Finely chop the garlic.

In a small bowl, combine the sugar, vinegar, and soy sauce; stir until the sugar has dissolved. Add the sliced and chopped ingredients. Spoon over the oysters and serve.

Japanese Lobster Rolls

SERVES 4
PREPARATION TIME: 30 MINUTES
CHILL FOR 20 MINUTES

1 daikon (Japanese white radish)
1 carrot
1 cup clover or alfalfa sprouts
3 scallions
2 tablespoons mayonnaise
1 teaspoon wasabi powder
$1/2$ teaspoon sesame oil
pinch salt
meat from $1^{1}/_{4}$ pound lobster
4 tablespoons sliced pickled ginger

PREPARATION

Peel the daikon and cut in half lengthwise. With a vegetable peeler or a mandolin, cut from the center (cut side) of each half at least 12 very thin slices measuring 6 inches long and 2 inches wide. The slices need to be thin—$1/16$ inch or less—so they will not crack when rolled.

Peel the carrot and cut it lengthwise into 4 slices about $1/8$ inch thick. Then cut each slice into strips and cut the strips into 4-inch-long pieces. Rinse and drain the sprouts. Trim the root end from the scallions. Otherwise, leave them whole.

Pour water into a medium skillet until it is a quarter full. Bring to a gentle boil over low heat and add the scallions. Let the water come back to a boil, then turn off the heat. Allow the scallions to stand in the hot water for 10 minutes.

In the meantime, whisk together the mayonnaise, wasabi powder, sesame oil, and salt. Cut the lobster meat into pieces about $1^{1}/2$ inches long.

Remove the cooked scallions from the water and gently slip the leaves apart, removing the outer ones first.

ASSEMBLY

Place a slice of daikon horizontally on a flat surface. Put $1/2$ teaspoon of the wasabi mixture in the center. Place 2 carrot sticks on top so they protrude over the top edge of the daikon. Place a small bunch of the sprouts on top of the carrot sticks, then arrange some of the lobster meat on top of the sprouts.

Starting from the left side of the slice of daikon, roll into a tight bundle, taking care that the daikon does not crack. Take one of the softened scallion leaves and tie it around the middle of each roll to hold it together.

Chill for 20 minutes. Garnish each serving with 1 tablespoon pickled ginger.

Crab & Chile Omelet

SERVES 4
COOKING TIME: 6 MINUTES

6 eggs
1 teaspoon salt
$1/2$ teaspoon freshly ground black pepper
8 ounces fresh crabmeat
4 scallions
2 fresh red chiles
1 tablespoon vegetable oil
1 teaspoon fish sauce

Beat the eggs, and season with the salt and pepper; set aside. Flake the crabmeat and remove any shell. Chop the scallions. Seed and finely slice the chiles.

COOKING

Heat 1½ teaspoons of the oil in a large skillet. Add the prepared scallions and chiles and cook for 1 to 2 minutes. Add the flaked crabmeat and the fish sauce. Stir well, and transfer the mixture to a bowl.

Wipe the skillet clean with a paper towel and place it over low heat. Add the remaining 1½ teaspoons oil. When it is warm, pour in the beaten eggs and cook until they are set on the bottom but still creamy on top. Spoon the crab mixture over half of the omelet and fold in half. Leave for 1 minute, then remove from the pan and serve.

Hoppers

These are made to be served with curry. Diners use the hoppers as "bread" to mop up and eat the sauce.

MAKES 12 (4 SERVINGS)
RISING TIME: 1 HOUR
COOKING TIME: 12 MINUTES

1 teaspoon active dried yeast
½ cup warm water
1½ teaspoons sugar
1½ cups rice flour
1½ cups all-purpose flour
1 teaspoon salt
2½ cups milk
2½ cups shredded coconut
2 cups hot water
vegetable oil, for wiping pan

PREPARATION

In a small saucepan, heat the milk until almost simmering. Make coconut milk by mixing in the shredded coconut and processing the mixture in a blender for 1 minute, then straining the liquid. Reserve the coconut and set aside the liquid to cool to lukewarm. Return the damp coconut to the blender and add the 2 cups of hot water. Blend, then strain and reserve this liquid separately.

Mix together the yeast, warm water, and sugar. Let stand for 10 minutes. The yeast should bubble and froth.

Meanwhile, in a large bowl mix together the 2 flours and the salt; set aside. Also, if you are using your oven as a warm spot for the batter to rise, heat the oven to 200° for 10 minutes, then turn it off.

hoppers

Down East we have our burger buns. The Sri Lankans have their hoppers (also known as appe). They are made and eaten mainly at breakfast, but they are also used to mop up curry or are eaten like a wrap into which small portions of fresh and cooked foods are placed. The way in which they are made in Sri Lanka involves a special curved pan, much like a small wok, and the use of hot coals. I've always made them using an omelet pan on a traditional stove.

When the first batch of coconut milk has cooled sufficiently, add it to the proofed yeast. Pour the yeast and coconut milk mixture into the flour mixture and stir to form a smooth, thick batter. Place in the slightly warm oven—or any other suitable warm place—for approximately 1 hour so that the yeast can work. The batter should double in volume. It should be of a thick, pourable consistency; add a little of the second batch of coconut milk to ensure that it is.

COOKING

Heat a large, heavy skillet over low heat. Wipe the pan with a little oil on a piece of paper towel. Pour in a ladle full of batter and swirl it around to create a thin, even coating. Cover the pan and cook for 5 minutes *without lifting the lid.*

When the top edges of the hopper just start to turn brown, it is ready. Remove from the pan and keep warm while repeating with the rest of the batter. Serve the hoppers warm with curries.

Eastern Vegetable Fritters

SERVES 6
COOKING TIME: 5 MINUTES

4 cups flour
2 teaspoons salt
3 cups water
1 teaspoon ground turmeric
2 teaspoons ground coriander
1 teaspoon cayenne pepper
3 teaspoons ground cumin
1 teaspoon chili powder
4 potatoes
1 fresh red chile
2 onions
quarter of a cauliflower
about 1 cup of 1 or 2 other vegetables
   (any combination)
half a small cucumber
8 cups oil, for deep-frying
3 tablespoons mango chutney

PREPARATION

Sift the flour into a large bowl. Stir in the salt, then slowly pour in the water. Mix thoroughly to a thick, pourable batter. Add the turmeric, coriander, cayenne, cumin, and chili powder; mix thoroughly.

Dice and parboil the potatoes. Seed and coarsely chop the chile. Coarsely chop the onions. Cut the cauliflower into small florets and parboil. Prepare the other vegetables of your choice and cut into 1-inch pieces. (Note: Any root vegetables need to be parboiled.)

Add all the prepared vegetables to the batter and mix well. Finely chop or grate the cucumber.

EASTERN VEGETABLE FRITTERS

COOKING

Heat the oil in a deep saucepan. When very hot, spoon in the batter mixture, 2 to 3 spoonfuls at a time, and cook until the fritters turn a light saffron color. Remove from the oil and drain thoroughly on paper towels.

Serve at once with the prepared cucumber and the mango chutney as accompaniments.

Japanese Marinated Mushrooms

SERVES 6
COOKING TIME: 1 MINUTE
MARINATE OVERNIGHT

36 small mushrooms
(any variety, or a combination)
1 small onion

2 tablespoons soy sauce
4 tablespoons white wine vinegar
3 tablespoons dry sherry
2 tablespoons sugar
1 teaspoon salt

PREPARATION

Wash and dry the mushrooms and remove the stems. Place the caps in a large bowl.

Mince the onion; combine it with the soy sauce, vinegar, sherry, sugar, and salt.

COOKING

Place the onion mixture in a saucepan over low heat. Bring to a boil, and cook for just 1 minute.

Pour the sauce over the mushroom caps, then place in the refrigerator to marinate overnight. Drain and serve.

soups & salads

Ginger & Saffron Seafood Broth

Use canned chicken broth for this recipe; it has the clarity that this dish requires.

SERVES 4
COOKING TIME: 30 MINUTES

**2 pounds mixed shellfish and fish fillets,
such as mussels, shrimp, scallops,
lobster tail, squid, cod, and flounder**
4-inch piece fresh ginger
a few chives for garnish
1 lemon
10 cups clear chicken broth
1/2 teaspoon freshly ground black pepper
good-sized pinch saffron threads

PREPARATION

Wash the seafood under cold running water. Cut and slice the fish fillets into large bite-sized pieces. Cut the squid into rings. Cut the lobster, if using, into pieces. (Note: Use only the tail portion of a fresh uncooked lobster; cut it into medallions with the shell left on.) Place all the seafood on a plate that will fit into a large steamer.

Slice the ginger. Wash and cut the chives into 6-inch lengths. Using a lemon zester, remove just the yellow layer of the lemon rind. Reserve this zest and the chives for garnish.

COOKING

Pour the chicken broth into a large saucepan. Add the ground pepper, ginger slices, and saffron. Place over medium heat and simmer gently for 20 minutes, then strain to remove the ginger and the saffron threads.

Return the broth to low heat while you steam the seafood. Start to warm 4 soup bowls.

Pour water into the steamer and bring it to a vigorous boil. When it is producing a good amount of steam, lower the plate of seafood into the steamer. Clamp on the lid and let steam for 3 to 4 minutes. Remove from the steamer and drain all the liquid from the plate.

Divide the seafood evenly among the warmed soup bowls, then pour the ginger-saffron broth over it. Garnish with the lemon zest and chives.

A Chowder from the Far East

SERVES 6
COOKING TIME: 30 MINUTES

1 onion
2 cloves garlic
1 tablespoon fish sauce
2 teaspoons sugar
4 tablespoons soy sauce
$1/2$ teaspoon freshly ground black pepper
2 teaspoons salt
1 teaspoon ground coriander
1 teaspoon chili powder
5 cups unsweetened coconut milk
4 cups chicken broth
1 pound waxy potatoes
1 pound uncooked shrimp
1 teaspoon sesame oil
1 teaspoon cornstarch

PREPARATION

Coarsely chop the onion and garlic. Place them in an electric blender with the fish sauce, sugar, 1 tablespoon of the soy sauce, the ground pepper, salt, coriander, and chili powder. Blend to a smooth paste. Pour into a saucepan and add the coconut milk and chicken broth.

Peel and cut the potatoes into small cubes. Peel and devein the shrimp; wash under cold running water, then chop.

COOKING

Bring the coconut milk mixture to a gentle simmer. Add the cubed potatoes, increase the heat, and boil gently until the potatoes are just cooked. If the soup becomes too thick, add a little water. Stir frequently to make sure the mixture doesn't stick to the bottom of the pan.

Add the chopped shrimp and continue to heat gently for 5 minutes, or until the chowder is almost at a simmer and the shrimp are cooked.

In a small saucepan, quickly heat the remaining 3 tablespoons soy sauce and the sesame oil. When the mixture just starts to simmer, blend the cornstarch with a little water and add to the pan. Whisk vigorously until the sauce just starts to thicken.

Serve the chowder in individual bowls and garnish with a dash of the soy-sesame sauce.

Ginger, Corn, & Chicken Soup

SERVES 6
COOKING TIME: 45 MINUTES

2-inch piece fresh ginger

1 small chicken

3 cups fresh corn cut from the cob,
   or 16-ounce can corn kernels

1 tablespoon dry sherry

1 egg

1 teaspoon salt

2 teaspoons cornstarch

PREPARATION
Coarsely chop the ginger.

COOKING
Place the chicken in a large saucepan. Add the chopped ginger and enough water to cover. Place over medium heat and bring to a boil, then reduce the heat and simmer for 30 minutes.

Remove the chicken and reserve the cooking stock. Cut all the meat from the bones. Remove and discard the bones and skin. Shred the meat.

Heat the corn with 6 cups of the cooking stock. Add the shredded chicken and the sherry. Simmer for 5 minutes. Whisk the egg with the salt; add to the soup and stir briskly.

In a small bowl, blend the cornstarch with a little water; add to the soup to thicken as necessary. Serve at once.

Sesame
Lobster Salad

SERVES 4
PREPARATION TIME: 15 MINUTES

1 pound cooked lobster meat,
  or the meat removed from two
  1¼-pound cooked lobsters
Chinese cabbage
daikon
1 carrot
1 fresh red bell pepper
1 cup chopped cilantro
cucumber
2 tablespoons sesame seeds
1 tablespoon soy sauce

juice from 1 lime
2 teaspoons sugar
2 teaspoons sesame oil

PREPARATION

Cut the lobster meat into presentable pieces; set aside.
Cut out the heart of the Chinese cabbage and slice
finely to yield 4 cups. Cut off a portion of the daikon;
peel and cut into matchstick-sized pieces to yield 1
cup. Cut the carrot into matchstick-sized pieces to
yield 1 cup. Seed and thinly slice the red bell pepper.
Peel the cucumber and cut into 8 or 12 thin slices.

COOKING

Place the sesame seeds in a small, heavy skillet over a
low heat. Toast them, stirring occasionally, until they

just start to turn golden brown. Remove from the heat the moment the color is reached.

ASSEMBLY

In a small bowl, combine the soy sauce, lime juice, sugar, and sesame oil; whisk until the sugar dissolves. In a large bowl, combine the sliced Chinese cabbage, daikon pieces, carrot pieces, and bell pepper slices. Pour the soy mixture onto the vegetables and toss together.

Divide the vegetable mixture among 4 salad bowls. Top with the lobster meat and garnish with the chopped cilantro, cucumber slices, and toasted sesame seeds.

Shrimp & Peanut Salad

SERVES 6
PREPARATION TIME: 10 MINUTES

2 small red onions
1 fresh green chile
1 green apple
1 cup bean sprouts
half a small head of lettuce
2 teaspoons sesame oil
2 teaspoons sugar
juice of 1 lime
2 pounds peeled cooked shrimp
1 cup dry roasted peanuts

PREPARATION

Mix together the sesame oil, sugar, and lime juice; stir until the sugar is dissolved.

Reserve a few of the heart leaves of the lettuce for garnish; shred the rest. Coarsely chop the onions. Seed the chile and cut into thin slices. Core and chop the apple, leaving the skin on.

Combine the onions, chile, apple, and shredded lettuce. Add the shrimp. Pour the sesame oil mixture over all and toss together. Sprinkle on the peanuts. Serve in individual salad bowls, garnished with the reserved lettuce leaves.

Cucumber & Shrimp Salad

SERVES 4
COOKING TIME: 5 MINUTES

half a seedless cucumber

1½ pounds peeled cooked shrimp

2 fresh red chiles

1 head romaine lettuce

3 tablespoons white wine vinegar

2 teaspoons sugar

1 teaspoon salt

PREPARATION

Thinly slice the cucumber. Seed and thinly slice the chiles.

Shred the lettuce and place in a salad bowl. Alternate the peeled shrimp and the cucumber slices around the edge of the bowl. Sprinkle with the chile slices and place the salad in the refrigerator.

COOKED DRESSING

In a small saucepan, gently heat the vinegar, sugar, and salt; stir constantly until the sugar is dissolved. Do not let the liquid come to a boil. Remove from the heat and chill in the refrigerator. When ready to serve, pour the vinegar mixture over the salad and serve.

Peanut, Shrimp, & Chicken Salad

SERVES 6
PREPARATION TIME: 20 MINUTES

2 medium carrots

1 cucumber

4 stalks celery

1 whole cooked chicken breast

4 sprigs mint

1 clove garlic

1 teaspoon oyster sauce

1 tablespoon rice vinegar

3 teaspoons sugar

4 teaspoons chili powder

$1/2$ pound peeled cooked shrimp

1 cup dry roasted peanuts

PREPARATION

Peel and thinly slice the carrots lengthwise, then cut into thin strips. Peel and slice the cucumber. Retain some center leaves of the celery for garnish; dice the rest. Shred the chicken breast meat. Chop the mint (leaves only; discard the stems).

Crush and finely chop the garlic. Place in a large bowl and add the oyster sauce, vinegar, sugar, and chili powder. Add the sliced carrots and cucumber and the diced celery.

Transfer the contents of the bowl to a serving dish and top with the shrimp, shredded chicken, and peanuts. Garnish with the reserved celery leaves.

Cooked Vegetable Salad

In Indonesia this is called gado gado. *Vegetables and salad items are boiled, parboiled, or mixed together fresh, with a rich peanut sauce as a dressing. Any combination of salad items and vegetables will work fine.*

SERVES 6
COOKING TIME: 40 MINUTES
ALLOW 1 HOUR FOR COOLING.

3 scallions
2 cups bean sprouts
half a small cucumber
2 stalks celery
½ pound fresh green beans
1 small cabbage heart
3 potatoes
2 carrots
3 eggs
4 fresh red chiles
3 cloves garlic
2 tablespoons vegetable oil

8-ounce jar crunchy peanut butter
4 cups unsweetened coconut milk
1 teaspoon sugar
2 teaspoons lemon juice

PREPARATION

Chop the scallions. Coarsely chop the cucumber. Finely chop the celery. Cut the beans diagonally. Shred the cabbage. Peel the potatoes and cut in half. Peel the carrots and cut into thin strips.

COOKING

Lightly boil the cut beans for 2 to 3 minutes; drain and set aside. Blanch the shredded cabbage. Boil the halved potatoes until cooked, then slice. Parboil the carrot strips. Hard-boil the eggs, then peel and cut into quarters. Place the prepared vegetables and eggs in refrigerator to chill.

Heat the oil in a small skillet. Add the chiles and cook for 3 to 4 minutes. Remove and drain. Add the garlic and cook in the same way.

Transfer the cooked chiles and garlic to an electric blender. Add the peanut butter, coconut milk, and sugar and blend until smooth. Pour the mixture into a small saucepan and add the lemon juice. Bring to a simmer and allow to thicken but still retain its pouring consistency. Refrigerate until cool.

ASSEMBLY

In a large serving bowl, toss together the bean sprouts, chopped cucumber, with the prepared green beans, cabbage, potatoes, and carrots. Pour on the peanut sauce. Garnish with the chopped celery, chopped scallions, and egg quarters.

Pagoda Crab Salad

SERVES 4

PREPARATION TIME: 15 MINUTES

1 bunch watercress

2 tomatoes

2 ripe avocados

½ pound crabmeat

1 fresh red chile

2 tablespoons Dijon-style mustard

1 shallot

2 cloves garlic

1 teaspoon white wine vinegar

2 egg yolks

3 tablespoons vegetable oil

PREPARATION

Note: This salad requires a 3-inch metal mold, which can be purchased from a good-quality kitchen shop or restaurant supply store. You can also make your own for no cost. Thoroughly rinse a 16- to 20-ounce food can (the type that typically contains pineapple chunks or baked beans). Using a traditional kitchen can opener, remove the top and the bottom to make a metal tube, which is an ideal mold.

Wash the watercress and chop enough to yield 2 cups. Remove the seeds from the tomatoes and cut the flesh into ¼-inch cubes. Remove the pit from the avocadoes; peel and chop the avocadoes into ¼-inch cubes. Pick over the crab and remove any remaining shell. Remove seeds from the chile.

Place the mustard, shallot, garlic, vinegar, seeded chile, and egg yolks in an electric blender and blend to a smooth paste. Drizzle in the oil a little at a time until the mixture is the consistency of mayonnaise.

ASSEMBLY

Coat the inside of the mold with a little of the oil. Place the mold on a serving plate. Press a quarter of the chopped watercress into the bottom of the mold. Add some chopped tomato, then chopped avocado. Press down firmly. Place a quarter of the crabmeat on top of the avocado and press down firmly again.

Carefully remove the mold by continuing to press firmly onto the crabmeat as you turn and lift off the mold. As the mold lifts away, reduce the pressure on the crabmeat. Repeat with the remaining ingredients until you have 4 towers. Garnish with some of the remaining tomato and avocado slices, then pour some of the mustard mixture over each salad before serving.

seafood

Barbecued Shrimp with Chile, Lime, & Mint

SERVES 4
COOKING TIME: 10 MINUTES

2 pounds large uncooked shrimp (preferably with the heads still on)
1 tablespoon vegetable oil
3 limes
1 fresh green chile
small bunch mint

PREPARATION

Either metal or bamboo skewers may be used for this recipe. Bamboo skewers should be soaked in cold water for an hour before using so the exposed ends are less likely to burn while grilling.

Push a skewer from the tail end of each shrimp up to the head. This keeps the shrimp straight while cooking and also ensures that the shrimp cook evenly. Rub the shrimp with some of the oil. Cut 2 of the limes into ¼-inch-thick slices. Pour the remaining oil over the sliced lime. Juice the third lime. Seed and thinly slice the chile. Pull the mint leaves from the stems.

COOKING

Place the skewered shrimp onto a hot grill and cook until the undersides of the shells turn red. Turn the shrimp and cook until they are completely done and the shells are all red. This should take only a minute or so. Avoid overcooking.

Meanwhile, place the oiled lime slices on the grill for the last minute or so and allow them to just start to brown. Remove the shrimp and the lime slices from the heat. Remove and discard the skewers.

Place the shrimp on a serving platter, pour the lime juice over them, and top with the grilled lime slices. Sprinkle with the sliced chile and garnish with the mint leaves.

NOTE: The shrimp can be eaten with their shells on, or you may prefer to peel them before eating. (The shells are considered a meal in themselves in many parts of Asia, and I sometimes serve them as a snack.)

Spicy Fried Shrimp

SERVES 4
COOKING TIME: 8 MINUTES

1 pound uncooked shrimp
1-inch piece fresh ginger
1 scallion
2 teaspoons Tabasco sauce
1 tablespoon tomato sauce
1 teaspoon soy sauce
2 teaspoons salt
½ teaspoon freshly ground black pepper
3 cups vegetable oil
1 tablespoon dry sherry

PREPARATION

Peel and devein the shrimp. Wash under cold running water, and dry thoroughly. Mince or finely chop together the ginger and scallion. Mix together the Tabasco sauce, tomato sauce, soy sauce, and the salt and pepper; set aside.

COOKING

Heat the oil in a wok or large, deep skillet. When the oil just starts to smoke, add the peeled shrimp and deep-fry until they are just cooked. Remove and drain thoroughly on paper towels.

Pour away most of the oil, leaving about 1 tablespoon to stir-fry. Add the ginger-scallion mixture and stir-fry for 1 minute. Add the cooked shrimp and continue to stir-fry for another minute. Sprinkle the shrimp mixture with the sherry, then pour in the sauce mixture. Stir for 1 minute, and serve immediately.

Maple Pepper Shrimp

SERVES 4
COOKING TIME: 10 MINUTES

1¹/₂ **pounds uncooked shrimp**
   (with shells on)

2 **medium yellow onions**

2 **tablespoons chicken broth**

1 **tablespoon lemon juice**

2 **teaspoons cornstarch**

3 **teaspoons freshly ground black pepper**

1 **teaspoon salt**

3 **tablespoons vegetable oil**

3 **tablespoons maple syrup**

PREPARATION

Peel and devein the shrimp. Wash under cold running water and pat dry. Slice the onions. Blend together the chicken broth, lemon juice, cornstarch, ground pepper, and salt.

COOKING

Heat the oil in a large, heavy skillet or wok. Add the peeled shrimp and the sliced onions; stir-fry for 4 minutes. Add the maple syrup and continue to stir-fry for 1 minute. Pour in the broth mixture and stir for another minute, then serve.

Chile, Shrimp, & Corn Fritters

SERVES 6

COOKING TIME: 15 MINUTES

4 cups corn kernels, preferably fresh

1 egg

2 tablespoons self-rising flour
   (or 2 tablespoons plain flour plus
   ¹/₂ teaspoon baking powder)

1 tablespoon water

1 red onion

2 cloves garlic

1 teaspoon salt

¹/₂ teaspoon freshly ground black pepper

1 teaspoon chili powder

¹/₂ pound peeled, uncooked shrimp

handful cilantro leaves and stalks

1 tablespoon vegetable oil

4 tablespoons sweet chile sauce
   (see page 21)

PREPARATION

Cook the corn in boiling water for 1 minute; remove, drain, and transfer to a bowl.

Beat the egg; add the flour and the water and mix thoroughly to eliminate any lumps. The batter should be of pouring consistency. Add more water if the batter is too dry. Pour the batter over the corn.

Finely chop the onion and garlic. Add to the corn along with the salt, pepper, and chili powder. Mix well; the batter should be thick.

Chop the shrimp and cilantro; add to the batter and stir to combine.

While in Singapore I was fortunate to have been taught a great deal about the food and cooking of the region, as well as the art of Nonya cooking, by Mrs. Lee Chin Koon, mother of Lee Kuan Yew, then prime minister of Singapore. (Nonya is the marriage of Chinese ingredients with the spices and traditions of Muslim Malaysia.)

We spent several days exploring the food markets and cooking in her kitchen, where she taught me some of her skills as a Nonya cook. Mrs. Lee is an authority on Nonya cooking and has written a book on the subject.

The highlight of the week was a late-night visit to Fat Albert's restaurant, where, according to Mrs. Lee, the very best Singapore Chile Crab was made by Fat Albert himself. Not only did Fat Albert cook and serve us this delicious dish, he took me into his kitchen, showed me how to prepare it, and gave me his recipe. This is my Down East version, using lobster rather than crab. With all due modesty, I think it's better than the master's.

COOKING

Heat the oil in a large, heavy skillet. Spoon in 3 to 4 tablespoons of the batter and allow to cook through and brown on one side. Turn and let brown on the other side. Transfer to paper towels to drain, then place in a warm oven. Repeat with the remaining batter. Serve with the Sweet Chile Sauce for accompaniment.

Down East Spicy Lobster

I use culls for this dish. Once you have cut up the lobsters, you can't tell that they were not perfect.

SERVES 4
COOKING TIME: 20 MINUTES

4 lobsters, 1¼ lb each,
    or the equivalent larger lobsters
1 egg
3 cloves garlic
4 fresh red chiles
1-inch piece fresh ginger
4 tablespoons tomato sauce
2 teaspoons sugar
1 teaspoon salt
2 teaspoons cornstarch
1 tablespoon vinegar
small bunch cilantro
1 tablespoon oil
1 cup chicken broth

DOWN EAST SPICY LOBSTER

PREPARATION

Kill the lobsters (see note), then thoroughly clean them and discard the inedible bits. Cut the lobster into manageable pieces. Crack the claws.

Beat the egg; set aside. Finely chop the garlic. In an electric blender, combine the chiles, ginger, tomato sauce, sugar, and salt. Add the cornstarch and vinegar and blend again for a few seconds. Coarsely chop the cilantro.

COOKING

Heat the oil in a very large skillet or wok. Add the chopped garlic and lobster pieces. Cook for 2 minutes, then pour in the chicken broth. Cover and let simmer for 15 minutes.

Add the chile mixture and the beaten egg. Stir continuously until the sauce thickens.

Serve in a large bowl with the chopped cilantro sprinkled on top.

NOTE: There are two methods for killing a lobster. The quicker and more humane approach is to insert a knife blade just behind the top of the head, then pull it forward. If you are not comfortable with this approach, you can drop the lobster into a pot of boiling water and cook it for 2 or 3 minutes or until the lobster stops moving, then plunge it into cold water and proceed with the recipe.

Grilled Thai Chile Lobster

SERVES 4
COOKING TIME: 30 MINUTES

4 cloves garlic

3 shallots

2 small fresh red chiles

2 small fresh green chiles

$1/2$ cup chopped cilantro

two 2-pound uncooked lobsters

2 tablespoons vegetable oil

2 tablespoons fish sauce

$1/2$ teaspoon freshly ground black pepper

PREPARATION

Finely slice the garlic and shallots. Seed and finely slice the red and green chiles. Coarsely chop the cilantro.

COOKING

Pour 3 to 4 inches of water into a very large pot; bring to a boil. Add the live lobsters and let the water return to a boil. Cook for 2 minutes, then remove from the heat and carefully pour away all but 1 inch of water. Return to the heat, place a lid to almost cover the pot, and steam the lobsters for 12 minutes. Remove the lobsters and allow them to cool long enough to handle.

Start a grill or broiler and get it up to a high heat. Cut the cooked lobsters in half, down the center of the back. Remove the claws; crack them open, remove all the meat, and cut it into bite-sized pieces. Clean out the body cavity and discard the inedible bits. Remove the tail meat from the shell and carefully slice it, taking care to keep the tail shell together. Return the tail meat to the shell. Place the cut-up claw meat into the body cavity.

Heat the oil in a small pan. Add the sliced garlic and cook gently, taking care not to burn it. As the garlic starts to brown, add the sliced shallots and chiles, the fish sauce, and the ground pepper. Stir and cook gently for a few seconds.

Spoon the chile mixture evenly over the 4 lobster halves. Place the lobsters on the preheated grill or under the broiler and cook for 3 to 4 minutes.

Transfer to 4 dinner plates and sprinkle with the chopped cilantro.

lessons from thailand

Thailand lies at the crossroads of Asia, halfway between India to the west and China to the east, yet it shares little with either when it comes to culinary skills and flavors. Rice is the staple food of Thailand, as it is in India and southern China, but that is where any similarity ends.

The food of Thailand is distinctively light, which makes it attractive to us in the West, with our current demands for flavorful, nutritious meals that do not burden our digestive system. With our busy lifestyles, we also want meals that are quick to prepare. Thai cooks have had the same demands made of them for centuries. Therefore, most meals are ready within a few minutes.

Without a doubt, the flavors and methods of cooking in Thailand have influenced me as a cook and are evident in many of the recipes on these pages.

Lobster Curry

SERVES 6
COOKING TIME: 1 HOUR 10 MINUTES

three 2-pound uncooked lobsters
4 yellow onions
5 cloves garlic
3-inch piece fresh ginger
$1/2$ pound green beans
2 teaspoons ground turmeric
2 teaspoons chili powder
1 teaspoon cumin seeds
4-inch cinnamon stick
1 teaspoon salt
3 cups coconut milk
3 tablespoons shredded coconut

3 tablespoons rice flour
juice of 2 lemons

PREPARATION

Kill the lobsters (page 53). Wash them thoroughly and cut them into serving portions. Remove and discard all the inedible bits. Crack the claws.

Chop the onions and garlic. Grate the ginger. Trim the beans and cut them into $1\frac{1}{2}$-inch-long pieces.

COOKING

In a very large, heavy saucepan or flameproof casserole, combine the chopped onion and garlic and grated ginger. To make the curry sauce, add the turmeric, chili powder, cumin seeds, cinnamon stick, and salt. Add 2 cups of the coconut milk and place the pan over medium heat. Bring the mixture to a boil, then reduce the heat, cover, and let simmer for 25 minutes.

In the meantime, toast the shredded coconut and rice flour in a dry pan over low heat until they just turn brown, stirring continuously to avoid burning.

Add the lobster pieces to the simmering curry sauce; simmer for another 10 minutes. Stir well to make sure the lobster pieces are well covered with the sauce at all times. Remove the lobster to a warm serving bowl and keep in a warm oven.

Transfer the browned shredded coconut and rice flour to an electric blender. Add the remaining 1 cup coconut milk; blend for a few seconds, then pour the mixture into the curry sauce.

Add the lemon juice to the curry sauce mixture. Stir well and simmer for another 10 minutes, then return the lobster pieces to the pan. Add the cut-up green beans. Stir and simmer for 5 more minutes. Remove the cinnamon stick, and serve.

curry

The ancient wise men of India believed that food is a gift from the gods, and its preparation is a form of prayer. Spices are freshly ground daily. Meat and vegetables are combined with spices, fruit, nuts, and lentils in a variety of ways, resulting in food that is diverse in color, texture, and taste.

Nowhere will you find curry powder in an Indian kitchen. In fact, you won't even find the word curry, *which is actually an eighteenth-century British creation that seems to have had its origins in the Tamil word* kahri, *which means sauce.*

This dish was inspired by a basic recipe from the southwestern Indian state of Kerala, where the preparation varies daily depending on the catch of local fish. I use whatever is the freshest at my local market. Quite often, coconut milk and yogurt are used together, and in many kitchens only the coconut milk is used. The all-coconut milk version tends to be much sweeter. The addition of chiles to the blended paste adds some real fire.

Seafood Curry

SERVES 6
COOKING TIME: 40 MINUTES

1 yellow onion

1 tart green apple

3 potatoes

2 tomatoes

3 pounds assorted white-fleshed fish fillets,
calamari, shrimp (uncooked, shell off),
and scallops

2 tablespoons vegetable oil

2 teaspoons salt

1/2 teaspoon freshly ground black pepper

1 teaspoon ground turmeric

1/2 teaspoon chili powder

1/2 teaspoon ground cinnamon

1/2 teaspoon ground cumin

1 teaspoon ground coriander

1 teaspoon flour

4 cups coconut milk

1 tablespoon lemon juice

PREPARATION

Peel and chop the onion and apple. Peel the potatoes
and cut into small cubes. Dice the tomatoes. Wash and
pat dry the seafood and cut it into bite-sized pieces.

COOKING

Heat the oil in a large, heavy pan. Add the chopped apple and onion and cook until the apple just starts to turn golden brown and the onions are transparent. Sprinkle on all the spices and the flour. Pour in the coconut milk; stir well and bring to a gentle boil, then reduce the heat and simmer for 30 minutes.

Add the diced tomatoes, the prepared seafood, and the lemon juice; stir carefully. Do not bring back to the boil, just let the fish cook gently for 3 to 4 minutes, taking care not to break up the fillets. Serve immediately.

Pepper Crab

Any type of fresh, live crabs will do, and local crabs in season are ideal. If crabs are not available, lobsters are just as good.

SERVES 6
COOKING TIME: 15 MINUTES

2 fresh red chiles

6 scallions

6 cloves garlic

4 teaspoons whole black peppercorns

6 uncooked crabs

3 tablespoons vegetable oil

parsley sprigs for garnish

PREPARATION

Seed and finely slice the chiles. Chop the scallions; crush the garlic and coarsely chop. Bruise the peppercorns by lightly crushing them on a chopping board under a heavy pan.

COOKING

Steam the crabs as you would lobsters, cooking them for 15 minutes.

Heat the oil in a small pan; add the chopped garlic and cook for 1 to 2 minutes, or until it just starts to brown. Add the chopped scallions and crushed peppercorns and continue cooking for 2 minutes.

Transfer the steamed crabs to a serving plate. Top with the hot oil containing the scallions, peppercorns, and garlic. Garnish with the slivers of chile and the parsley.

To eat, crack open the crabs and dip the meat into the spicy pepper oil.

Steamed Basil & Mussels

This dish needs fresh holy basil, which is not easy to find outside of Asian markets. If you are unsuccessful, you can substitute regular sweet basil, but it doesn't have the distinctive anise fragrance that holy basil imparts. If you use sweet basil, add 3 or 4 whole star anise. The other key ingredient is galangal, which is found in Asian markets, but ginger can be substituted in this dish.

SERVES 4
COOKING TIME: 5 MINUTES

2 pounds farm-raised fresh mussels
2 stalks lemongrass
   (about 6 to 8 inches long)
3-inch piece galangal or fresh ginger
5 cups water
generous bunch holy basil

Dipping Sauce

2 cloves garlic
1 fresh red chile
juice of half a lemon
1 tablespoon soy sauce
2 teaspoons sugar
2 tablespoons fish sauce

PREPARATION

Remove any beards from the mussels, and discard any mussels with broken shells. Wash thoroughly under cold running water.

Chop the lemongrass into 2-inch-long pieces. Cut the galangal into 1-inch pieces. Pour the water into a large pot and add the basil and chopped lemongrass and galangal.

To make the Dipping Sauce, chop the garlic very finely. Seed and finely chop the chile. Combine the chopped garlic and chile with the lemon juice, soy sauce, sugar, and fish sauce. Pour into a dipping bowl.

COOKING

Place the pot with the aromatics and the water over high heat. Cover and quickly bring the mixture to a boil. Add the prepared mussels and clamp the lid back on. Steam vigorously until all the mussels are open. Strain the contents of the pot through a colander to remove the liquid. Serve the mussels immediately with the Dipping Sauce.

PREPARATION

Wash the scallops under cold running water; drain and pat dry. Finely grate the ginger; combine it with the sherry and soy sauce. Add the prepared scallops and let marinate for 3 minutes.

Beat the eggs. Put the cornstarch in a large bowl and add the beaten eggs, the water, and the salt and pepper. Beat together to form a batter. Slice the lemon for garnish.

COOKING

Heat the oil in a wok or deep skillet. Remove the scallops from the marinade and dip them into the batter, making sure they are well coated. Then put them into the hot oil and cook until they are golden brown. Remove, drain, and serve garnished with the lemon slices.

Marinated Fried Sea Scallops

SERVES 6
COOKING TIME: 10 MINUTES

1 pound large sea scallops
2-inch piece fresh ginger
2 tablespoons dry sherry
2 tablespoons soy sauce
2 eggs
1/2 cup cornstarch
3 tablespoons water
1 teaspoon salt
1/2 teaspoon freshly ground black pepper
1 lemon
3 cups vegetable oil

Salmon with Ginger Maple Soy Sauce

SERVES 4
COOKING TIME: 35 MINUTES

1¹/₂ pounds salmon fillets

1 teaspoon salt

1 teaspoon freshly ground black pepper

1 teaspoon cayenne pepper

1 lime

1 tablespoon vegetable oil

PREPARATION

Wash the fillets under cold running water, removing any skin, bones, or scales. Pat dry, then sprinkle with the salt, ground pepper, and cayenne. Slice the lime for garnish.

COOKING

Heat the oil in a large, heavy skillet. Add the seasoned fillets. Cook gently on one side until the fish is almost cooked through. Turn the fillets and cook for a minute or two more.

Transfer the fillets to 4 dinner plates. Pour some Ginger Maple Soy Sauce (recipe follows, page 65) over each. Garnish with lime slices and serve.

Ginger Maple Soy Sauce

2-inch piece fresh ginger

3 cloves garlic

2 tablespoons vegetable oil

1 cup soy sauce

2 tablespoons maple syrup

PREPARATION

Peel the ginger and finely chop. Crush the garlic and finely chop.

COOKING

Heat the oil in a small, heavy saucepan over low heat. Add the chopped garlic and ginger and cook gently for 2 to 3 minutes. Add the soy sauce and bring to a slow boil. Add the maple syrup and continue to boil until the volume is reduced by about one third and the sauce has a thick consistency.

Steamed Ginger Fish

SERVES 6

COOKING TIME: 10 MINUTES

1 whole white-fleshed fish, 3 to 5 pounds

5 scallions

2 portabella mushrooms

3 slices bacon

3-inch piece fresh ginger

1 tablespoon butter

1 cup chicken broth

1 tablespoon soy sauce

1 teaspoon dry sherry

1 teaspoon cornstarch

1 teaspoon salt

1 head of lettuce

1 lemon

1 fresh red chile

2 teaspoons vegetable oil

PREPARATION

Clean the fish, making sure that all the scales have been removed. Leave the skin on. Remove the head if you wish. Wash the fish thoroughly under cold running water. Dry carefully with a paper towel.

Place 2 of the scallions on a plate that will fit into a steamer. Place the fish on top.

Slice the mushrooms. Coarsely chop the bacon. Peel the ginger and slice it as thin as possible. Arrange the sliced mushrooms, chopped bacon, and sliced ginger on top of the fish. Dot the top with butter, then place the plate in the steamer.

Mix together the chicken broth, soy sauce, sherry, cornstarch, and salt. Finely shred the lettuce. Finely slice the yellow zest from the lemon and cut into thin matchstick pieces. Seed the chile and cut it into thin slices. Slice the remaining 3 scallions lengthwise into thin strips.

GINGER FLOWER

STEAMED GINGER FISH

COOKING

Steam the fish over very high heat for 7 to 10 minutes. Drain the fish and remove and discard the mushrooms, bacon, and ginger. Place the fish on a warm plate and cover with aluminum foil to keep it warm.

In a small pan, heat the oil. Add the broth mixture; stir and bring quickly to a boil.

Arrange the shredded lettuce on a large serving platter. Place the steamed fish on top and garnish with the strips of lemon zest, the thinly sliced chile, and the scallion strips. Pour the hot broth mixture over the fish and serve immediately.

Fish Fillets with Spicy Yogurt & Potato Sauce

SERVES 4
COOKING TIME: 35 MINUTES

2 pounds fish fillets (cod or halibut)
1 teaspoon ground turmeric
1 teaspoon salt
4 yellow onions
10 cloves garlic
2 cups plain yogurt
1 teaspoon freshly ground black pepper
1 teaspoon cayenne pepper
1 teaspoon maple syrup
11 tablespoons (total) vegetable oil
3 potatoes
8 whole cardamom pods
three 2-inch cinnamon sticks

PREPARATION

Wash the fish under cold running water. Remove any skin, bones, or scales. Pat dry, then sprinkle with the turmeric and salt.

Finely chop 2 of the onions. Quarter the other two and place in an electric blender. Add the garlic, yogurt, ground pepper, cayenne, maple syrup, and 2 table-spoons of the oil. Blend to a smooth paste. Peel the potatoes and chop into half-inch cubes. Crush the cardamom pod so the seeds can just be seen.

COOKING

Heat 6 tablespoons of the remaining oil in a large, heavy skillet. Add the fish fillets and cook for 3 to 4 minutes on each side, taking care not to break them when you turn them over. They should be nicely crisp and brown. Remove them from the pan and place on paper towels to drain.

Pour the remaining 3 tablespoons oil into the pan. Add the finely chopped onions, chopped potatoes, crushed cardamom pods, and cinnamon sticks. Cook until the onions just turn brown. Reduce the heat and pour in the yogurt mixture. Simmer gently for 10 minutes, or until the potatoes are just cooked, stirring occasionally.

Remove and discard the cinnamon sticks and cardamom pods. Remove the fish and keep warm. Pour the cooking liquid into a food processor and blend to a smooth sauce. If the mixture seems too dry, add a little water. Return the sauce to the pan and heat gently. Add the fish fillets and allow to heat through before serving.

chicken
duck & quail

Tea-Smoked Duck

Chinese cooking is all about flavor and texture, and this dish has it all. The cooked duck is smoked for flavor, then "cooked" again briefly in hot oil to give the skin a crisp, crunchy texture. This recipe must be started at least a whole day before you plan to serve it.

SERVES 4 TO 6

COOKING TIME: 1.5 HOURS, PLUS 2 HOURS
  TO COOL

1 large duck, about 6 pounds

2 teaspoons salt

1 tablespoon freshly ground black pepper

1 cup loose tea leaves

1 cup rice flour

1 cup sugar

10 cups vegetable oil

parsley, for garnish

PREPARATION

Clean and remove any excess fat from the duck. Rub the duck inside and out with the salt and ground pepper. Wrap the seasoned duck in aluminum foil and refrigerate it for 24 hours.

COOKING

Remove the duck from the refrigerator; rinse and pat dry. Place the duck in a suitable steamer, and steam over boiling water for 1½ hours.

In the meantime, line a large wok or deep pan with aluminum foil. The pan should have a close-fitting lid.

Mix together the tea leaves, rice flour, and sugar; sprinkle the mixture over the foil. Place a metal rack on top of the foil so that the duck can rest about 2 inches above the bottom of the pan and directly above the tea-leaf mixture.

Place the steamed duck on its back on the rack and cover the pan. Dampen 2 tea towels and arrange them around the rim of the pan to keep smoke from escaping. Place the pan over high heat. The heat will make the tea smoke and give the duck its distinctive flavor.

Smoke the duck in this fashion for 10 minutes over high heat, then reduce the heat to low and smoke the duck for 20 minutes more. Remove the pan from the heat and let the duck rest in the pan until the smoke completely disperses. Then remove the duck from the pan and let cool on a plate, covered with a tea towel, for about 2 hours at room temperature.

Heat the oil in a large wok or large, deep pan. (If you use a large pan, you may need more oil.) When the oil is hot, carefully lower the duck into it. Spoon the hot oil continuously over the duck for 8 minutes, then transfer the duck to a rack and let it drain thoroughly. Place it on a serving plate, garnish with the parsley, and serve immediately.

Duck Breasts with Thai Curry Sauce

Duck breasts vary greatly in size, but in general men will eat two breast portions, while women manage one.

SERVES 4
COOKING TIME: 20 MINUTES

3 or 4 whole duck breasts
3 cloves garlic
1 small yellow onion
2 tablespoons vegetable oil
1 tablespoon Massaman curry paste
  (see Curry Pastes next page)
2 cups chicken stock

PREPARATION

Separate the whole breasts into serving portions by cutting through the skin that joins the two halves. Keeping the skin intact on each portion, trim off any excess skin and fat. With a sharp knife, score the skin on each breast in a crisscross pattern; the scores should be about half an inch apart. Finely chop the garlic and onion.

COOKING

Warm the oil in a medium-sized, heavy saucepan over medium heat. Add the chopped garlic and onion. Cook gently until the onion is just soft, then add the curry paste. Stir well and continue to cook for 2 minutes more.

Add the chicken stock and bring to a boil. Stir well, reduce the heat, and let simmer for 15 minutes.

Remove the pan from the heat and allow the curry sauce mixture to cool a little. Then pour it into a food processor or an electric blender and process to a smooth consistency. Return the mixture to the pan and keep it warm over low heat. Do not allow it to boil.

Preheat the oven to 400° F.

Place a heavy, ovenproof skillet over high heat. When the pan is very hot, add the duck breasts, skin side down. Cook for 2 to 3 minutes, or until the skin is brown and has rendered a lot of fat. Turn the breasts and continue to cook for 2 minutes more.

Remove the pan from the stove top and place in the preheated oven. Let the duck continue to cook for 6 to 8 minutes.

Remove the duck breasts from the pan and place on paper towels to drain. Transfer the duck breasts to serving plates and pour the warm curry sauce over them. Serve.

curry pastes

Supermarkets and specialty food stores now carry curry pastes from India and Thailand. The pastes, made from blended spices, ginger, garlic, onions, tomato paste, and oils, are wonderfully simple and convenient. The Indian varieties come in glass jars and are easy to reseal and store. The Thai versions come in tins; once they are opened, the contents need to be packed into suitable storage jars, though they do not need to be refrigerated.

The most popular Indian pastes are mild, medium, or hot. Other styles, which are harder to find, include Vindaloo, Masala, Balti, Tandoori, Tikka, Madras, Rogan Josh, Jalfrezi, and Korma.

The most popular Thai pastes include red, green, yellow, and Massaman. The red is very hot; the green is relatively hot, and the yellow is somewhat milder. The Massaman is even milder but has a complex flavor base.

Like many classic dishes from around the world, Beggar's Chicken has a colorful story about how it came into being, if indeed it is true. History books do not record such facts. Regardless, this is how, according to cooking legend, Beggar's Chicken got its name.

A hundred years ago, a homeless beggar committed a serious crime. He stole a chicken from a farmer and ran off into the countryside, with the farmer and his wife in hot pursuit. Driven by his fear, the beggar outran his victims. He eventually came to a river, where he was able to hide in the rushes. Frightened by the thought of what would happen to him if he were caught with the evidence, he decided to hide the chicken by burying it in the mud on the bank of the river. He left the chicken there and returned in the dark of the night to retrieve his booty. By this time, the sun had baked the mud so it totally encased the chicken.

The beggar threw the caked chicken onto a fire, more out of disgust than an attempt to cook it. As the fire died down and only embers remained, the beggar could smell the wonderful aroma of freshly baked chicken. Much to his surprise and delight, the chicken had cooked in its mud casket and had split open in the searing heat of the embers. He broke away the baked-on mud and enjoyed the succulent bird.

Today this dish is prepared throughout southern China and is served to guests with a hammer with which to break open the clay crust. It is easily prepared in your own home with modeling clay from a craft supply store.

Beggar's Chicken

SERVES 6
COOKING TIME: 2 1/2 HOURS

This dish uses a thick flour-paste casing to keep all the juices and flavors in the chicken. You can use modeling clay instead of the flour paste. If you do, add another 45 minutes to the cooking time.

6 large mushrooms
large dill pickle
1 onion
1/2 pound bacon
1 chicken, about 4 pounds
3 pounds (9 cups) flour
2 teaspoons vegetable oil
2 teaspoons soy sauce
2 teaspoons dry sherry
2 teaspoons sugar
1 teaspoon freshly ground black pepper
14 large outer cabbage leaves

PREPARATION

Chop the mushrooms, pickle, and onion. Dice the bacon. Wash the chicken and pat dry. Mix the flour with enough water to make a very stiff paste. Preheat the oven to 375° F.

COOKING

Heat the oil in a large, heavy skillet. Add the diced bacon and stir-fry for 10 minutes. Add the chopped mushrooms, pickles, and onion and stir-fry for 5 minutes longer. Add the soy sauce, sherry, sugar, and ground pepper. Stir-fry for another 2 minutes, then set aside to cool.

Stuff the cavity of the chicken with the bacon mixture. Close the cavity with a small metal skewer or by sewing it with a coarse thread. Wrap the chicken in 10 of the cabbage leaves, reserving 4 of the leaves for garnish.

Cover the wrapped chicken with the thick flour paste, making sure there are no cracks or holes, which would allow the juices to escape. Place the encased chicken on a large sheet of aluminum foil, then loosely bring up the edges and crimp them together to form a dish around the chicken.

Place the chicken, inside its foil dish, in a baking pan. Place the pan in the preheated oven and bake for 2 hours. Remove the pan from the oven, break open the casing, and remove and discard the cabbage leaves. Spoon the bacon mixture out of the chicken and onto a plate

Place the 4 reserved cabbage leaves on a serving platter. Top with the broken casing. Arrange the cooked chicken and the bacon mixture on top. Serve.

Dry Chicken &
Coconut Curry

SERVES 4
COOKING TIME: 45 MINUTES

2 whole boneless chicken breasts

4 onions

3 cloves garlic

2 tablespoons butter, softened

$1/2$ teaspoon ground cumin

1 teaspoon ground coriander

1 teaspoon ground turmeric

1 teaspoon ground ginger

$1/2$ teaspoon chili powder

1 teaspoon freshly ground black pepper

2 teaspoons salt

2 teaspoons white wine vinegar

2 tablespoons vegetable oil

1 tablespoon tomato paste

juice of 1 lemon

3 tablespoons shredded coconut

PREPARATION

Cut the chicken into bite-sized pieces. Slice the onions very finely. Crush and chop the garlic. Place the softened butter in a small bowl and add the spices, salt, and vinegar. Blend thoroughly and set aside.

COOKING

Heat the oil in a large, heavy skillet. Add the sliced onions and chopped garlic and cook for 5 minutes. Remove the pan from the heat. Transfer the cooked onions and garlic to the spice mixture. Add the tomato paste, stir to combine, then return the mixture to the pan and cook for 5 minutes longer.

Add the chicken pieces to the pan. Stir well so that the spice mixture coats all the chicken. Cover the pan and simmer gently until the chicken is tender. Uncover occasionally to make sure the chicken is not burning. If it looks as though it might, add a little water, but no more than 2 to 3 tablespoons at a time.

When the chicken is tender, add the lemon juice and shredded coconut. Stir well, and cook for 1 to 2 minutes more before serving.

Asparagus & Walnut Chicken

SERVES 4
COOKING TIME: 20 MINUTES

2 whole boneless chicken breasts

6 small mushrooms

1 teaspoon soy sauce

1 tablespoon dry sherry

1 tablespoon cornstarch

$1/2$ pound asparagus

1 clove garlic

2 tablespoons vegetable oil

4 ounces shelled walnuts

2 tablespoons oyster sauce

PREPARATION

Dice the chicken breasts. Slice the mushrooms. Mix together the soy sauce, sherry, and cornstarch. Pour this mixture over the diced chicken and stir well. Cut the asparagus into 1-inch lengths. Crush the garlic.

COOKING

Heat the oil in a large pan or wok over high heat. Add the crushed garlic and cook until it is golden brown, then discard. Add the chicken mixture to the pan and stir-fry. When the chicken is just cooked, add the walnuts, sliced mushrooms, and asparagus pieces. Continue to stir-fry. Pour in the oyster sauce and stir-fry for 2 minutes more.

Steamed Chicken & Tomatoes

SERVES 4
COOKING TIME: 30 MINUTES

2 whole boneless chicken breasts

4 tomatoes

4 scallions

1-inch piece fresh ginger

2 tablespoons fish sauce

1 teaspoon chili powder

1 teaspoon salt

4 teaspoons freshly ground black pepper

1 teaspoon sugar

2 teaspoons vegetable oil

PREPARATION

Cut the chicken into bite-sized pieces. Cut the tomatoes into quarters. Finely chop the scallions and grate the ginger.

Place the chicken pieces and quartered tomatoes in a bowl that will fit inside a large saucepan and is suitable for steaming. Combine all the other ingredients and pour over the chicken and tomatoes. Seal the bowl with plastic wrap to seal in the flavor and prevent excess moisture from getting into the food.

COOKING

Place the bowl in a deep saucepan, and pour enough water into the pan to come halfway up the bowl. Cover the pan, place over high heat, and let the chicken steam for 30 minutes, or until it is tender.

Grilled Skewered Ginger Chicken

SERVES 6
COOKING TIME: 12 MINUTES

1 small cucumber

1/2 cup sweet sherry

1/2 cup soy sauce

2 tablespoons sugar

2 whole boneless chicken breasts

3 teaspoons ground ginger

PREPARATION

Grate the cucumber, peel and all, and set aside. Make a marinade by mixing together the sherry, soy sauce, and sugar and stirring until the sugar dissolves.

Cut the chicken into bite-sized pieces and place on small metal or bamboo skewers. Allow 3 or 4 skewers per person. Place the skewers on a large, flat, shallow dish. Pour the marinade over the chicken, and let stand for 15 minutes. Turn over once or twice to make sure the chicken is thoroughly coated with the marinade.

COOKING

Preheat the grill or broiler to medium heat. Cook the chicken for 3 to 4 minutes per side. Remove from the heat, brush with the remaining marinade, and sprinkle with the ground ginger. Return the chicken to the heat and cook for another 1 to 2 minutes, or until the chicken is tender but not dry. Garnish with the grated cucumber and serve.

GRILLED SKEWERED GINGER CHICKEN

Asparagus
& Quail Curry

SERVES 6
COOKING TIME: 1 HOUR

2 large onions

6 cloves garlic

one 16-ounce can peeled tomatoes

¹⁄₂ pound asparagus

6 quail

6 slices bacon

2 tablespoons ground turmeric

2 tablespoons vegetable oil

1 tablespoon medium-hot curry paste

1 cup chicken broth

1 teaspoon salt

juice of 1 lemon

PREPARATION

Slice the onions very finely. Crush and chop the garlic. Chop the tomatoes. Cut the asparagus into 2-inch-long pieces. Preheat the oven to 450° F.

COOKING

Place the quail in a roasting pan breast side up. Cover each bird with a slice of bacon. Place the pan in the preheated oven and cook the quail for 20 minutes. Remove the pan from the oven and dust the birds with half of the turmeric.

Heat the oil in a large, heavy skillet over medium heat. Add the sliced onions and chopped garlic and cook until they are golden brown. Add the remaining turmeric and the curry paste. Stir-fry for 2 to 3 minutes, then add the chopped tomatoes and chicken broth. Stir well, reduce the heat, and simmer gently for 20 minutes.

Add the roasted quail; cover the pan and simmer for an additional 5 minutes. Add the prepared asparagus and simmer, uncovered, for 5 minutes more. Sprinkle with the salt and lemon juice. Stir well and serve.

beef, pork & lamb

Far East Burgers

SERVES 4
COOKING TIME: 12 MINUTES

10 mint leaves
half a lemon
1 stalk lemongrass
1 small red onion
1 tomato
2 fresh red chiles
1 clove garlic
1 lime
1 pound ground sirloin or lean hamburger
1 egg
1 tablespoon fish sauce
1 tablespoon Thai curry paste
   (preferably red)
1 tablespoon vegetable oil
4 pita bread pockets
salad greens
mango chutney

PREPARATION

Chop the mint leaves. Using a lemon zester, remove just the yellow layer of the lemon rind. Finely chop the white bulb end of the lemongrass stalk. Halve the onion; cut one half into slices, and chop the other half. Slice the tomato. Seed and thinly slice the chiles. Finely chop the garlic. Squeeze the juice from the lime.

Combine the ground beef, the egg, and the chopped mint, zest, and lemongrass. Add the chopped onion, lime juice, fish sauce, chopped chiles and garlic, and curry paste. Shape the mixture into 4 burger-sized patties.

COOKING

Heat the oil in a heavy skillet over medium heat. Cook the burgers until they are just brown on one side. Turn over and continue cooking until they are done to your liking.

Warm the pita bread pockets in a toaster oven or under the broiler. Place an onion slice, a tomato slice, a few greens, and a cooked burger inside each one, and top with the mango chutney. Serve with the remaining salad greens and tomato and onion slices.

Bombay Meatballs

SERVES 6
COOKING TIME: 10 MINUTES

1 pound ground sirloin

1 small yellow onion

3 cloves garlic

1½ teaspoons chili powder

2 eggs

1 tablespoon ground coriander

1 teaspoon ground cumin

1 tablespoon soy sauce

1 tablespoon brown sugar

juice of 1 lemon

8 cups vegetable oil

PREPARATION

Place the ground beef in a large bowl. Finely chop the onion and garlic and add to the meat. Sprinkle with the chili powder. Lightly beat the eggs and add to the bowl together with the coriander, cumin, soy sauce, brown sugar, and lemon juice. Mix thoroughly, then form into golf ball–sized meatballs with your hands.

COOKING

Heat the oil in a deep saucepan until just smoking. Cook the meatballs a few at a time until golden brown. Drain thoroughly on paper towels, and serve either hot or cold.

Japanese Hot Pot

SERVES 4
COOKING TIME: AT TABLE

Dipping Sauce

3 tablespoons sesame seeds
2 cups chicken broth
1 teaspoon chili powder
3 tablespoons soy sauce
1 tablespoon rice vinegar

Hot Pot

2 pounds sirloin steak
4 scallions
8 ounces bean sprouts
6 medium mushrooms
1 cabbage heart
8 ounces extra-firm tofu
8 cups chicken broth
1 teaspoon salt
$1/2$ teaspoon freshly ground black pepper

PREPARATION

To make the Dipping Sauce, toast the sesame seeds in a heavy skillet over medium heat until they start to pop. Transfer them to a grinder or blender and grind to a fine powder. Place them in a bowl and add the chicken broth, chili powder, soy sauce, and vinegar. Stir well, then pour into 4 individual dipping bowls.

the japanese garden

As a visitor to Japan studying the eating and cooking habits of the people, I observed one outstanding feature of the country's cuisine that I personally try to emulate when serving meals to my friends.

That feature is the artistry with which the food is prepared and presented. A Japanese meal needs a quiet room overlooking a tranquil garden with appropriate flower arrangements placed in the right positions. The serving plates, bowls, and platters harmonize with the colors and textures of the season. And then there's the food: sculptured, carved, and garnished with flowers and leaves. In spring, small pink cherry blossoms fashioned out of tofu float in your bowl of miso. In summer, green fans cut from cucumbers, and butterflies from lemon slices, grace a simple fish steak.

In Japan, much of your meal is eaten with your eyes. I've designed my dining room on this very simple idea. Guests can sit at my table and enjoy the New England seasonal changes in my "Japanese garden"—including koi, bonsai, and delicate Japanese maples—while they eat food garnished simply to reflect the time of year.

Cut the steak into thin slices by semi-freezing the meat and using a very sharp knife. Diagonally slice the scallions into 2-inch lengths. Wash the bean sprouts. Cut the mushrooms in half. Remove the tough outer leaves from the cabbage and cut the cabbage heart into bite-sized pieces. Drain the tofu and cut into bite-sized pieces. Arrange plates of mixed vegetables and meat, allowing 1 plate for 2 people.

COOKING

Heat the chicken broth in a large fondue pot over medium heat. When the broth simmers, adjust the seasoning with the salt and ground pepper. Place the fondue pot on a table burner in the center of the table. Arrange the plates of meat and vegetables around the pot. Give each guest a small bowl of Dipping Sauce.

Each guest, with chopsticks or a fondue fork, dips a piece of meat or vegetable into the simmering stock and cooks it, one piece at a time. Each piece is then dipped into the sauce and eaten. You may wish to supply additional dipping sauces: soy sauce, horse-radish, or chile. When all the meat and vegetables are eaten, the stock is then served as soup.

Chile Rib Eye Steak with Salad & Cucumber-Mint Chutney

SERVES 4
COOKING TIME: 10 MINUTES

2 teaspoons freshly ground black pepper

1 tablespoon crushed dried chiles

1 teaspoon chili powder

2 large rib eye steaks,
    about 2 1/2 pounds total weight

1/2 pound mixed salad greens

half a seedless cucumber

15 mint leaves

1 large tomato

1 red bell pepper

1 pound fresh bean sprouts

2 tablespoons soy sauce

juice of 1 lime

2 teaspoons sugar

2 teaspoons sesame oil

PREPARATION

Mix together the ground pepper and crushed dried chiles and chili powder; spread the mixture on a dinner plate.

Trim any excess fat from the steaks. Press each side of each steak into the seasonings to form a thick coating; set aside.

Wash the salad greens. Grate the cucumber, peel and all, and finely chop the mint leaves. Mix the grated cucumber and chopped mint together; set aside.

Wash the bean sprouts. Cut the tomato in quarters and then chop each quarter into thirds. Cut the bell pepper in half, remove the seeds, and cut each half into 8 pieces.

To make the salad dressing, combine the soy sauce, lime juice, sugar, and sesame oil; stir until the sugar dissolves. Set aside.

COOKING

Heat a griddle or a heavy, cast-iron skillet until it is very hot. Place the steaks in the dry pan and cook for 4 minutes, then turn over and continue to cook to the desired doneness.

Meanwhile, toss the washed salad greens with the bean sprouts, tomato, bell pepper, and the dressing, and place on 4 dinner plates. Remove the steaks from the heat; let stand for a couple of minutes, then slice the meat and arrange it on the greens. Serve with the cucumber-mint chutney on the side.

Chinese Pepper Steak

SERVES 4
COOKING TIME: 25 MINUTES

2 pounds sirloin steak tips
3 onions
4 cloves garlic
3 teaspoons freshly ground black pepper
2 tablespoons sugar
5 tablespoons soy sauce
3 medium tomatoes
2 tablespoons butter
1 teaspoon vegetable oil
2 teaspoons ground cinnamon

PREPARATION

Beat the steak flat with a meat mallet or rolling pin. Coarsely chop one of the onions. Cut the garlic cloves in half. Place the chopped onion and halved garlic in an electric blender and add the ground pepper, sugar, and soy sauce; blend to a smooth paste.

Coat the flattened steak with the paste and let marinate for 1 hour at room temperature. In the meantime, finely slice the remaining 2 onions. Peel and chop the tomatoes.

COOKING

In a large skillet over medium heat, melt the butter. Just as it starts to froth, add the oil. Add the sliced onions and cook until just transparent. Add the steak and all the marinade. Cook until the steak starts to brown, stirring occasionally.

Add the cinnamon and the chopped tomatoes to the pan. Continue to cook for 1 minute, then pour in enough boiling water to just cover the steak. Reduce the heat and let simmer, uncovered, until most of the liquid has evaporated and the steak is tender. Serve immediately.

Braised Lamb Shanks with Asian Spices

SERVES 6
COOKING TIME: 3 HOURS

6 cloves garlic
3 yellow onions
2 tablespoons vegetable oil
2 tablespoons ground cumin
2 teaspoons ground coriander
1 tablespoon paprika
1 tablespoon ground turmeric
1 teaspoon ground cinnamon
2 teaspoons ground ginger
2 teaspoons crushed red chiles
3 to 6 lamb shanks (depending on size)
one 28-ounce can peeled tomatoes

PREPARATION

Crush and chop the garlic. Peel and thinly slice the onions. Preheat the oven to 250° F.

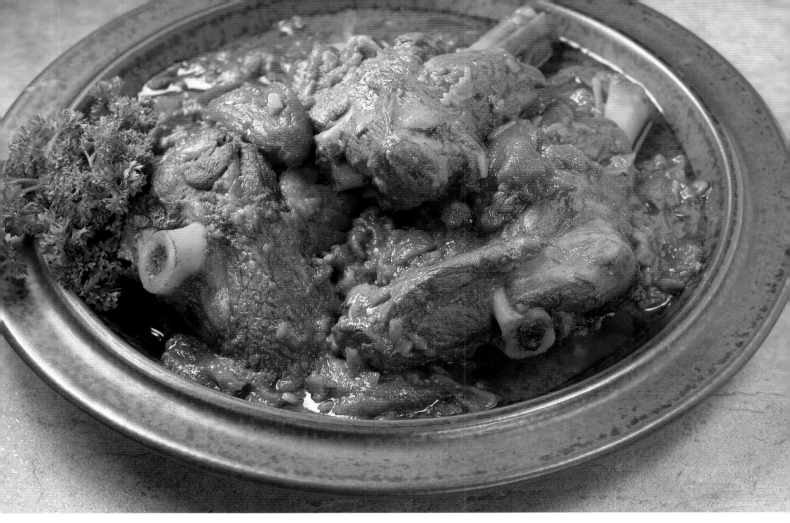

BRAISED LAMB SHANKS WITH ASIAN SPICES

COOKING

Place a large, cast-iron or other flameproof casserole over low heat. The pot should have a tight-fitting lid. Pour in the oil. Let it warm for a minute, then add the chopped garlic and sliced onions. Cook until the onions just start to brown. Add all the spices and the chiles. Stir well and continue to cook for 2 minutes, stirring once or twice.

Add the lamb shanks, turning so they just start to brown on all sides. Add the tomatoes and cover with the tight-fitting lid. Place the casserole in the preheated oven and let the lamb slowly braise. Gently stir the contents every 30 minutes. Allow to cook until the meat is almost falling off the bone—about 3 hours.

Remove the meat from the casserole, transfer it to a large platter, and serve with all the cooking juices and vegetables.

Sweet Garlic Pork

SERVES 4
COOKING TIME: 25 MINUTES

1½ pounds pork tenderloin

2 teaspoons salt

1 teaspoon freshly ground black pepper

½ cup flour

2 onions

3 cloves garlic

4 scallions

4 tablespoons vegetable oil

1 cup chicken broth

3 teaspoons tomato paste

3 tablespoons brown sugar

2 tablespoons soy sauce

PREPARATION

Cut the pork in thin slices (about ¼ inch). Sprinkle with the salt, pepper, and flour and set aside. Finely chop the onions and garlic. Coarsely chop the green part of the scallions; set aside.

COOKING

Heat 2 tablespoons of the oil in a large, heavy skillet. Add the seasoned and floured pork and cook until golden brown. Remove from the pan, drain on paper towels, and set aside.

Pour the remaining 2 tablespoons of oil into the pan. Add the chopped onions and garlic, and cook until the onions are just transparent. Add the chicken broth, tomato paste, and brown sugar. Stir well and cook for 1 to 2 minutes.

Reduce the heat and return the cooked pork to the pan. Add the soy sauce and continue to cook for 10 minutes. Increase the heat and cook for about 5 minutes, by which time all the liquid should be absorbed. Garnish with the chopped scallions and serve.

Lettuce-Wrapped Pork Packets

SERVES 4
COOKING TIME: 10 MINUTES.

1 head iceberg lettuce

8 ounces bean sprouts

4 scallions

2 tomatoes

1½ pounds pork tenderloin

3 cloves garlic

1 small yellow onion

1 tablespoon vegetable oil

1 teaspoon crushed red chiles

1 teaspoon ground cumin

1 teaspoon salt

½ teaspoon freshly ground black pepper

PREPARATION

Cut the core out of the lettuce and pull away all the leaves, taking care to keep them intact. Carefully wash the lettuce leaves and let dry.

Wash the bean sprouts. Chop the scallions and tomatoes; set aside. Mince or very finely chop the pork. Crush and chop the garlic. Peel and finely chop the onion.

COOKING

Heat a wok or large, heavy skillet over high heat. Pour in the oil. After about 30 seconds, add the chopped garlic and onion. Stir-fry for 2 to 3 minutes, then add the chopped pork and continue to cook for another 2 to 3 minutes. Add the crushed red chiles, cumin, salt, and ground pepper. Continue to stir-fry until the pork is cooked to your liking.

Arrange the pork on a serving plate. Serve with separate dishes of the washed bean sprouts, chopped scallions, chopped tomatoes, and lettuce leaves. Guests take a lettuce leaf, place some bean sprouts inside, spoon in the pork, and top it with the chopped scallions and tomatoes. The lettuce leaf is then wrapped into a packet and eaten with the fingers.

vegetables &rice

GINGER STEWED TOMATOES

Ginger Stewed Tomatoes

Locally grown tomatoes picked at peak ripeness are the best for this recipe.

SERVES 4
COOKING TIME: 30 MINUTES

8 large tomatoes
2 cloves garlic
2-inch piece fresh ginger
1 onion
4 tablespoons vegetable oil
$^1/_2$ teaspoon salt
1 teaspoon chili powder
1 tablespoon sugar

PREPARATION

Cut the tomatoes in half horizontally. Finely chop the garlic and ginger. Finely slice the onion.

COOKING

Heat the oil in a large, heavy skillet over a medium to low heat. Add the chopped garlic and ginger and the sliced onion. Cook for 5 minutes, then add the tomato halves, cut side up, and cook for 10 minutes.

Sprinkle the tomatoes with the salt, chili powder, and sugar. Turn the tomatoes so the cut surface is now in the hot oil. Lower the heat and continue to cook for 15 minutes, or until the liquid has evaporated and the edges of the tomatoes start to turn brown. Serve at once.

Indian Fried Potatoes & Onion

SERVES 6
COOKING TIME: 35 MINUTES

1 large onion
6 medium waxy potatoes
1 fresh red chile
3 tablespoons vegetable oil
$^1/_2$ teaspoon cumin seeds
$^1/_2$ teaspoon mustard seeds
2 teaspoons salt
1 tablespoon Garam Masala curry powder
juice of 1 lemon
parsley

PREPARATION

Peel and coarsely chop the onion. Peel and halve the potatoes. Seed and finely chop the chile.

COOKING

Boil the halved potatoes until just soft, then drain and mash them; set aside.

Heat the oil in a large, heavy skillet over medium heat. Add the cumin and mustard seeds. Cook for 1 minute, then add the chopped chile. Continue to cook for another minute, then add the chopped onion. Cook for 5 minutes, then add the mashed potatoes, salt, Garam Masala, and lemon juice. Stir-fry for 7 minutes. Serve garnished with the parsley.

Cucumber Relish

SERVES 6
COOKING TIME: 10 MINUTES
CHILL: 2 HOURS

3 small cucumbers
1 onion
2 cloves garlic
1 fresh green chile
1 teaspoon ground ginger
½ teaspoon chili powder
1 teaspoon salt
2 tablespoons vegetable oil
juice of 1 lemon

PREPARATION

Peel and coarsely chop the cucumbers. Finely chop the onion and garlic. Seed and finely chop the chile.

COOKING

Place the chopped cucumber in enough water to just cover, and boil for 10 minutes. Drain thoroughly and transfer to a small bowl.

Add the chopped onion, garlic, and chile to the bowl. Mix well, then add the ground ginger, chili powder, salt, oil, and lemon juice. Stir to combine, then refrigerate for at least 2 hours before serving.

Green Vegetables & Coconut Curry

SERVES 6
COOKING TIME: 12 MINUTES

1½ pounds mixed green vegetables
   that are in season, such as green beans,
   snow peas, and green bell peppers
3 fresh green chiles
1 onion
2 tablespoons peanut oil
1 cup shredded coconut
good-sized pinch saffron threads
1 cup water
1 tablespoon freshly squeezed lemon juice
1 teaspoon salt

PREPARATION

Wash the mixed green vegetables; coarsely chop or shred the larger ones. Leave small vegetables whole. Seed and finely slice the chiles. Finely slice the onion.

COOKING

Heat the oil in a large, heavy skillet. Add the sliced chiles and cook for 5 minutes.

Pour off most of the oil, then add the prepared mixed green vegetables, the sliced onion, ¾ of the coconut, the saffron, and the water. Cover and cook for 5 minutes. Add the lemon juice and salt. Stir and cook, uncovered, for 2 minutes. Sprinkle with the remaining coconut and serve at once.

GREEN VEGETABLES & COCONUT CURRY

Mushroom Curry

SERVES 6
COOKING TIME: 30 MINUTES

3 onions
12 ounces mushrooms
1 tablespoon butter
1 tablespoon tomato paste
1 teaspoon ground cumin
1 teaspoon ground cloves
1 tablespoon hot water
1 cup plain yogurt
2 cups chicken broth
2 teaspoons salt
1 teaspoon freshly ground black pepper
1 teaspoon chili powder

PREPARATION

Finely chop the onions. Slice the mushrooms.

COOKING

In a large, heavy skillet, melt the butter. Add the chopped onions and cook until golden brown. Add the tomato paste, cumin, and cloves. Cook, stirring, for 4 to 5 minutes, then add the sliced mushrooms and the hot water. Continue to cook for another 5 minutes, then add the yogurt, chicken broth, salt, ground pepper, and chili powder. Stir well, then simmer for 15 minutes. Serve hot.

Vegetable & Spice Stuffed Eggplant

SERVES 4
COOKING TIME: 45 MINUTES

2 cups cooked mixed vegetables, such as potatoes, onions, celery, and carrots (leftovers are ideal)
2 large eggplants
1 onion
3 cloves garlic
3 fresh green chiles
1 tablespoon butter
1 teaspoon ground turmeric
2 teaspoons ground coriander
2 teaspoons ground cumin
4 teaspoons ground cardamom
½ teaspoon ground cloves
4 teaspoons ground ginger
2 teaspoons salt

PREPARATION

Chop all the cooked vegetables. Cut the eggplant in half lengthwise and scoop out the center. Retain the skins. Finely chop the onion. Crush and chop the garlic. Seed and finely chop the chiles.

COOKING

Place the eggplant flesh in a large pot. Add water and simmer until soft, then drain. Chop and mix with the other chopped vegetables.

VEGETABLE & SPICE STUFFED EGGPLANT

Heat the butter in a heavy skillet. Add the chopped onion, garlic, and chiles. Cook until the onion turns golden brown. Add the turmeric, coriander, cumin, cardamom, cloves, and ginger. Continue cooking for a few minutes, then add the chopped mixed vegetables and the chopped eggplant. Add the salt and mix thoroughly.

Stuff each half eggplant skin with the cooked mixture. Place in a steamer and steam for about 20 minutes, or until the eggplant is completely tender. Serve immediately.

Coconut Rice

SERVES 6
COOKING TIME: 20 MINUTES

1 pound (2½ cups) long-grain rice
half a lemon
3½ cups coconut milk
1 teaspoon salt

PREPARATION
Wash the rice under cold running water until the water runs clear. Grate the zest of the half lemon very finely.

COOKING
In a saucepan with a tight-fitting lid, combine the coconut milk, grated zest, and salt and bring to a boil. Add the washed rice; cover the pan loosely and let boil for about 10 minutes, or until steam starts to escape through holes in the surface of the rice. Reduce the heat as low as possible, cover tightly, and leave for another 10 minutes before serving.

desserts

COC0NUT & BANANA PUFFS

Coconut & Banana Puffs

YIELD: APPROXIMATELY 36 PUFFS
(ABOUT 6 SERVINGS)
COOKING TIME: 10 MINUTES

16-oz. packet spring roll wrappers (about 6" square)
3 ripe bananas
4 tablespoons shredded coconut
milk, for moistening pastry
6 cups peanut oil
2 tablespoons confectioners' sugar

PREPARATION

With a round 3-inch cookie cutter, cut 2 circles from each spring roll wrapper.

Peel the bananas and mash them into a bowl. Mix in the shredded coconut.

Place about half a tablespoonful of the banana mixture on half of each pastry circle. Moisten the edges of the pastry with a little milk, then fold the other half of the pastry over the banana mixture to form a half circle. Crimp the edges with a fork to seal them.

COOKING

Heat the oil in a deep saucepan. When very hot, carefully drop in the pastries. Deep-fry for 20 to 30 seconds, or until golden brown. Drain thoroughly on paper towels, then dust with the confectioners' sugar. Serve either hot or cold.

Coconut Pudding

SERVES 6
COOKING TIME: 45 MINUTES
CHILL FOR 1 HOUR

3 tablespoons butter
6 eggs
1 cup sugar
5 teaspoons flour
1 teaspoon ground cinnamon
2 cups unsweetened coconut milk

PREPARATION

Preheat the oven to 375°F. Butter a large ovenproof bowl or 6 individual custard cups.

Separate the eggs and set aside the whites. In the bowl of an electric mixer, beat the butter and sugar to a smooth consistency. Add the flour and cinnamon and mix well.

Add the egg yolks to the bowl one at a time and continue to beat until the mixture is light and fluffy. Gently add the coconut milk and beat again.

Beat the egg whites separately until very stiff, then fold into the mixture.

COOKING

Pour the mixture into the buttered bowl or individual custard cups and place in a deep baking pan. Pour enough hot water into the pan to come three quarters of the way up the bowl or cups. Place the pan in the preheated oven and bake for 45 minutes.

Remove the pan from the oven. Chill the custard in the refrigerator for 1 hour before serving.

Almond Mallow

SERVES 6
COOKING TIME: 5 MINUTES
CHILL: 2 HOURS

3 cups water

6 teaspoons unflavored gelatin

1 cup sugar

¹/₂ cup evaporated milk

1 teaspoon almond extract

whole strawberries for garnish

mint leaves for garnish

COOKING

Bring the water to a boil and add the gelatin. Stir constantly until the gelatin dissolves. Add the sugar and continue to stir until it dissolves.

Remove from the heat and pour the liquid into a flat dish or a pan such as a jelly-roll pan. Add the evaporated milk and almond extract and stir. Refrigerate until set.

When firm, cut into bite-sized pieces and arrange in individual dishes. Garnish with the strawberries and mint.

Chinese Sesame Candied Apples

SERVES 6
COOKING TIME: 10 MINUTES

4 firm apples
1 cup self-rising flour
   (or 1 cup plain flour plus
   ½ teaspoon baking powder)
3½ cups water
8 cups peanut oil
1½ cups granulated sugar
1 cup sesame seeds
large bowl of ice water

PREPARATION

Peel, core, and cut each apple into 6 pieces. Sift the flour into a large bowl. Gradually add 3 cups of the water, stirring continuously. Add 1 teaspoon of the oil to the batter and mix thoroughly.

Add the apple pieces to the batter and stir to coat them thoroughly.

COOKING

Mix together the sugar and the remaining ½ cup water in a small sauce pan. Place over medium heat and bring to a gentle boil. Add the sesame seeds. Keep warm.

While the sugar syrup is heating, pour the remaining oil in a wok or large, deep pan and heat it until very hot. Drop in the coated apple pieces one at a time and deep-fry until they are golden brown. Remove and drain on paper towels.

Pour the oil from the skillet and rinse it out. Add the hot sugar syrup. Return the skillet to the heat and bring the syrup to a boil. Remove the pan from the heat.

Add the deep-fried apple pieces to the pan and turn to coat them thoroughly with the syrup. Quickly transfer the apple pieces to a serving plate. Dip each coated apple piece into the ice water, which will cause the soft syrup to turn brittle. This last stage must be done quickly to avoid very sticky results. Serve immediately.

Pavlova

*Strictly speaking, this dessert has no connection with
the Far East. It originated in New Zealand. However, it is
an excellent way to combine Asian fruits with such local
favorites as fresh blueberries.*

SERVES 6 GENEROUSLY
COOKING TIME: 1¹⁄₂ HOURS

6 egg whites

1¹⁄₄ cups sugar, plus more if desired

2 teaspoons cornstarch

1 teaspoon white wine vinegar

2 teaspoons vanilla extract

1 teaspoon butter

1¹⁄₂ cups heavy cream

1 pound fresh fruits and berries

PREPARATION

Preheat the oven to 300°F. Line a large baking pan with aluminum foil. Mark a 9-inch circle on the foil. Smear the circle and at least 2 inches outside it with the butter.

In the bowl of an electric mixer, beat the egg whites until they are stiff and form peaks. With the motor running, gently add the sugar and cornstarch. Leave to beat together for 1 minute. Add the vinegar and 1 teaspoon of the vanilla. Beat for half a minute more.

Spoon the egg white mixture into the middle of the buttered circle on the foil. With a rubber spatula, spread the mixture inside the mark. The "pile" of egg whites will be 3 to 4 inches high. Make an indentation on the top about an inch in from the rim and about an inch deep. Later, you will fill this with the heavy cream and fruit.

COOKING

Place the baking pan in the preheated oven and leave for 1 hour. Then turn off the oven and leave the pan there for another half an hour.

Remove the pan from the oven and let cool. If you are not going to serve the Pavlova within 1 hour, place it in a large airtight container.

When ready to serve, whip the heavy cream. Sweeten it with sugar and the remaining teaspoon vanilla, if desired. Pile the cream into the well in the meringue and garnish it artistically with the fresh fruit and berries.

anna pavlova and the pav

The creation of the "Pav," as this dish is known in New Zealand and Australia, dates back to 1926. The first recorded version was made in New Zealand; it has evolved into a dessert that is baked by almost every woman in both countries. Its origin has been fought over by chefs and food writers for decades on both sides of the Tasman Sea. The first serious research into the subject was undertaken by the University of Otago four years ago, when documented proof was discovered that clearly placed the country of origin as New Zealand and identified the name Pavlova given to the dessert in 1933.

Russian ballerina Anna Pavlova had toured New Zealand and Australia in 1926, and died shortly after, in 1931. The light and fluffy texture of the meringue-like base of the dessert looked like the tutu-style costume that Pavlova appeared in throughout her tour. Who first called the dessert "Pav" or "Pavlova" is unknown, but what can no longer be disputed is that the dish is truly a Kiwi-inspired creation.

HONEY WALNUTS &
VANILLA ICE CREAM

Honey Walnuts & Vanilla Ice Cream

SERVES 6
COOKING TIME: 15 MINUTES

4 tablespoons honey

3 teaspoons sugar

2 tablespoons peanut oil

4 ounces shelled walnut halves

2 teaspoons cornstarch

vanilla ice cream

PREPARATION

In a small bowl combine the honey and sugar.

COOKING

Heat the oil in a heavy pan or wok. Add the walnuts and cook until they just start to turn brown.

Remove the nuts from the pan and discard the oil. Return the nuts to the pan and add the blended honey and sugar. Stir well.

In a small bowl mix the cornstarch with a little water; add to the pan. Continue to stir until the nut mixture thickens. Serve at once over the ice cream.

Indian Almond Cheesecake

SERVES 6
COOKING TIME: 20 MINUTES
TOTAL COOLING/CHILLING TIME: 90 MINUTES

¼ cup blanched almonds

1 tablespoon butter

10 cups whole milk

juice of 1 lemon

8 tablespoons sugar

2 egg yolks

6 sprigs mint for garnish

PREPARATION

Chop the almonds coarsely. Butter a shallow oven-proof dish approximately 6" in diameter and 1½" to 2" deep. Sprinkle the bottom of the dish with the chopped almonds. Preheat the oven to 350°F.

COOKING

Place the milk in a large saucepan and bring it slowly to a boil. Add the lemon juice; stir and remove from the heat. Allow the curdled milk to cool for about 30 minutes.

Strain the cooled milk and place the curd in an electric blender. Add the sugar and egg yolks; blend until smooth.

Pour the blended mixture into the dish on top of the almonds. Place the dish in the preheated oven and bake for 15 minutes, or until set.

Remove the dish from the oven and allow to cool, then chill thoroughly (one hour or more). To serve, slide a sharp knife around the sides of the dish to loosen, then turn the cake out of the dish, with the chopped almonds now on top. Cut into 6 even slices and garnish with sprigs of mint before serving.

Coconut Custard with Raspberry Sauce

SERVES 6
COOKING TIME: 40 MINUTES
CHILL FOR 1 HOUR

4 eggs
2 cups sugar, divided
pinch salt
2 cups coconut milk
2 tablespoons shredded coconut
2 cups fresh raspberries
1 cup water
1 cup heavy cream
mint sprigs for garnish

PREPARATION

Preheat the oven to 350˚.

To make the custard, in a large bowl beat together the eggs, 1 cup of the sugar, and the salt until light and frothy. Add the coconut milk and stir well.

Pour the mixture into 6 individual bowls or 1 large bowl. Place in a shallow pan of hot water. Cover the bowls with aluminum foil.

COOKING

Place the pan with the bowls in the preheated oven and bake for 40 minutes, or until the custard is set. Remove from the oven and allow to cool, then place in refrigerator for 1 hour.

Meanwhile, place the shredded coconut in a small, heavy pan over medium heat. Toast the coconut gently, stirring frequently, until it is golden brown. Transfer the coconut to a plate and let cool.

To make the raspberry sauce, combine the berries, the remaining 1 cup sugar, and the water in a heavy pan over medium heat. Bring to a gentle boil, then lower the heat and let simmer for 4 to 5 minutes, stirring occasionally to make sure all the sugar is dissolved.

Pour the raspberry sauce through a sieve to remove all the seeds. Place the sauce in the refrigerator to cool completely.

Turn out the individual custards, or scoop some onto 6 serving plates. Sprinkle with the toasted coconut. Pour some of the raspberry sauce around the custard, and drizzle a little cream on top of the sauce. Garnish the custard with the mint sprigs and serve.

Blueberries, Sticky Rice & Custard

This recipe must be started the day before you plan to serve it. Soaking the rice overnight and then steaming it creates the desired chewy consistency.

SERVES 6
SOAKING TIME: 8 HOURS OR OVERNIGHT
COOKING TIME: 30 MINUTES
COOLING TIME: 45 MINUTES

3 cups sticky rice (sometimes labeled as sweet rice or glutinous rice)

2 cups unsweetened coconut milk

2 tablespoons sugar

coconut custard (see Coconut Custard with Raspberry Sauce, page 106)

½ pint fresh blueberries

PREPARATION

Soak the rice in cold water for at least 8 hours, or preferably overnight. Then wash the rice under cold running water until the water runs clear.

Prepare the custard as described on page 106, baking it in 1 large bowl.

COOKING

Line a steamer with cheesecloth. Place the washed rice on the cheesecloth and fold the loose ends over the rice. Cover the steamer and place it over gently boiling water. Steam the rice for 30 minutes. Let cool to room temperature.

In the meantime, bring the coconut milk to a gentle simmer. Add the sugar and stir until it dissolves. Set aside.

Transfer the steamed rice to a large bowl and pour in the coconut milk mixture. Stir to combine, then leave to cool to room temperature.

For each serving, divide the custard among individual bowls. Top the custard with a spoonful of the rice. Sprinkle with the fresh blueberries.

index